# Hollywood and the Professor
## *"The Flea's Reprieve"*

*A true story about my Dad
going viral in the 80s*

Written by Albert E. Millar, Jr., Ph.D.

Foreword by daughter, Heather E. Millar, Ph.D.

PUBLISHED BY MILLAR STRATEGIES, LLC

RICHMOND, VIRGINIA

This book was written over 40 years ago and is being published posthumously. The content depicts a true story and real events and was drawn from a variety of sources, including published materials and interviews. The views and opinions expressed in the story are those of the author only.

Copyright © 2024 by Heather E. Millar, Ph.D., MBA

All rights reserved. No part of this book may be reproduced in any form or by any means without the proper written consent of the author or publisher.

ISBN:9798991914727; LCCN: 2024923608

December 2024

Published by Millar Strategies, LLC

RICHMOND, VIRGINIA

*Dedicated to the family and students of the late
Dr. Albert E. Millar, Jr. (Dad)*

Valerie and Brian Butcher
Alyssa Cirrincione
Jacob Cirrincione
Cynara Colbert
Chloe Dupuis
Ginger and Mike Dupuis
Noah and Leeann Dupuis
Victoria M. Millar
Lauren (Dupuis), Jonathan and Elias Palmer

## FOREWORD

I was six years old and remember taking my blankie with me to the movie theater so my Dad could watch *E.T. the Extra-Terrestrial* for the second (or third?) time. I was old enough to know that my Dad really liked the movie but too young to appreciate why reporters started lining up outside of our home around that time. The term "going viral" did not exist in the early 1980s, but that's what was happening. My Dad went viral in the 80s.

My sisters and I lost our dad to cancer almost 25 years ago in 2000. He was the most senior professor at the time teaching in the English Department at Christopher Newport University. He had career-long interests in early American literature, the writings of Edgar Allen Poe and the Bible as literature. He also taught various survey courses in British, American and world literature.

He was beloved by students and colleagues alike. Nearly 25 years later, we still hear from his students telling us how much they loved him and how much of an impact he had on their lives. He was 59 when he passed from a hard fight with cancer, leaving behind thousands of students he taught over 33 years.

He also left behind an unpublished manuscript about his experience "going viral" and how Hollywood threatened to sue him over a little pamphlet he wrote called, "*E.T.*"—*You're More than a Movie Star,* a small pamphlet describing parallels he found between E.T. and the depiction of Jesus found in the Bible.

In a special double issue of *People* magazine in 1983, the article, "E.T., Short on Looks (But not Loving Fans), An Alien Finds His Home in Hollywood" mentioned Dad. "For some, like English professor Albert Millar Jr., 41, of Christopher Newport College in Virginia, the movie is a quasi-religious parable. Citing E.T.'s resurrection, his powers of healing and 31 other points, Millar has published a pamphlet, titled *"E.T."—You're More than a Movie Star,* comparing the alien's adventures to the story of Christ."

The ever-eccentric English professor who loved driving around with his oxymoronic license plate of "Poe Doc," he simply couldn't help himself when he saw the movie and began to see similarities between E.T. and Jesus/the Bible. He wanted to share the astonishing parallels he found with those he felt might be interested. In 1983, he took out advertisements for his pamphlet in the *New York Times,* and the *National Enquirer,* saying, "I never expected to make money, I just wanted to get people to read what I had written." He only asked for $1 each to help cover costs of printing and postage.

He was initially interviewed by *The Daily Press,* the local newspaper in Newport News, Virginia, and as they say, the rest is history. In the Christopher Newport University's (CNU) campus newsletter, *The Captain's Log,* they interviewed my Dad about what was perhaps one of the most celebrated media events in CNU's history:

"Dr. Millar, in 1982, independently published a pamphlet entitled *"E.T."—You're More than a Movie Star* drawing the ire from the lawyers at Steven Spielberg's studio, Universal City. Following an interview in *The Daily Press,* Universal City studios sent a telegram threatening legal action for trademark infringement and unfair competition. Dr. Millar's plight was then chronicled in the *Richmond Times-Dispatch, The Washington Post* and *News-*

*week* magazine. CBS radio did an interview with him, followed by a mention on *Entertainment Tonight*. *Saturday Night Live* also did small segments on the imbroglio and contacted him about doing a skit on the subject. Asked what he [Dad] thought about the studio's attempt at legal retribution, 'It's like using an atomic bomb to kill a flea.'" One of my favorite mentions is a comic strip from *Ziggy*.

Even Ed McMahon sent a letter of support for his cause. Speilberg stated he was neutral on the matter, despite the studio's objection, "I was born Jewish, I grew to become an atheist, and I don't know anything about this Jesus thing."

News outlets all over the country (and beyond!) were talking about the saga including the *Los Angeles Herald, Star, The LA Times, USA Today,* NPR, and a German wire-service. Talk shows mentioned it in California, Salt Lake City, Texas, Orlando, and Toronto. There was also a television spot for Cable News, on BBC, and a spot on ABC's *Good Morning America.*

Dad wrote a book at the time about his experience "going viral" entitled, *The Flea's Reprieve.* He said publishers didn't want to touch it at the time for fear of retribution from Hollywood. Since he passed away in 2000, I kept the handwritten and typed copies of his book, and I decided to publish his story in honor of the 25th year of his passing.

Despite never having smoked or consumed alcohol, our dad was given just a 5% chance of survival when he was diagnosed with stage-four bladder cancer on his 58th birthday, January 13, 1999. Faced with the worst possible prognosis, he chose to fight. In his 33 years of teaching, he never missed a class until he had to take a semester off for cancer treatment. In an article from *The Captain's Log* dated February 1, 1999, he expressed his feelings about this break, saying, "I have not missed a class in 33 years. Primarily, I feel guilty."

Dad was Chairman of the English Department at CNU from 1979-1986 and received numerous "Teacher of the Year" awards. He received his Bachelor of Arts from the University of Richmond, a Master's of English from the University of South Carolina, and a Doctorate in English from the University of Delaware.

My sisters and I miss him deeply. While we grieve losing him at such a young age, his memory lives on through our memories and his students—and now, through his book.

*– Heather E. Millar*

## CHAPTER ONE
## "The Bomb"

*"It's like using an atomic bomb to kill a flea."*
*The Associated Press, September 26, 1982.*

With this quotation, it felt like I was publicly born. I also discovered that the distance between a reporter's interview in the Newport News, Virginia, *The Daily Press* and an international news service is quite tiny.

On the day Linda Griffith came to my office in Christopher Newport Hall on the campus where I teach, I believed that her ensuing article may offer a small number of Virginians (60, 000 readership) a few details about a pamphlet that I had hurriedly written in July 1982 after taking my children to see *E.T. the Extra-Terrestrial* (Spielberg, 1982). I spoke with her for close to two hours explaining that someone who is trained to teach literature, as well as the Bible, just might have a certain predisposition for analogies or parallels when viewing other artistic productions, movies included. Also, I explained to her that I, as essentially a medievalist and a specialist in early American literature, had not the slightest desire to observe science fiction. Fantasy maybe — but science fiction, no.

As the interview proceeded, I subsequently felt the need to explain to Ms. Griffith that I might have had a more peculiarly attuned mind-set due to my status as the son and grandson of lay ministers in the fundamental Plymouth Brethren assembly. Whatever the impulses, I sat through the movie, so I continued to tell her, enthralled at the diverse emotional levels which Mr. Spielberg's creation induced in me, my family, and a packed theater in the Riverdale Shopping Center of Hampton, Virginia.

The impact of the movie instantly rivaled anything I had previously experienced, including my favorable response to *Lawrence of Arabia,* both *Godfathers,* and *Annie Hall.* For I had begun feasting on certain films in past years probably as result of the deprivation I felt in high school where I had attended a total of only two movies, *The Robe* and *The Ten Commandments.* But nothing, absolutely nothing hit me quite so powerfully as the underlying Christian atmosphere which so stunningly underscored the main character, E.T. All this, Ms. Griffith seemed to be absorbing until the interview was completed. With her statement that the succeeding Sunday paper would carry the article, we pleasantly bid our adieus.

And on the very next day, Tuesday, September 21, 1982, I opened my mailbox on campus to find a startling telegram from MCA-Universal City Studios accusing (even condemning) me of several violations of copyright laws. Only the actual telegram can reveal the magnitude of the problems I now realized were mine. And all due to a four-and-a-half-page pamphlet called *"E.T."—You're More Than a Movie Star* with my 33 parallels between the character and Jesus. In reading the telegram, I was receiving my initial and only contact from anyone associated with the movie. It speaks for itself.

Being the recipient of such a message can be appreciated only by those who have also been threatened by a lawsuit. Several special features of the telegram rang clearly through my

# HOLLYWOOD AND THE PROFESSOR: THE FLEA'S REPRIEVE

MIDDLETOWN, VA. 22645

**western union Mailgram**

1-028038M263 09/20/82 TLX MUSICOR UVSL NFKD
467 MCA INC, UNIVERSAL CITY, CA 15:10 PDT 09-20

DR. ALBERT E. MILLAR, JR./
CHRISTOPHER NEWPORT COLLEGE
50 SHOE LANE
NEWPRT NEWS VA  23606

MSG TR667
UNIVERSAL CITY STUDIOS, INC. IS THE OWNER OF ALL PROPRIETARY
RIGHTS TO THE MOTION PICTURE, "E.T. THE EXTRA-TERRESTRIAL",
INCLUDING BUT NOT LIMITED TO ALL CHARACTERS, CHARACTERIZATIONS,
COPYRIGHTS, TRADEMARKS, TRADE NAMES AND SERVICE MARKS RELATING
THERETO. WE HAVE BEEN ADVISED THAT YOU ARE SELLING E.T. BOOKLETS.
SUCH SALES ARE WITHOUT OUR CONSENT, PERMISSION OR AUTHORIZATION
AND INFRINGE UPON THE PROPRIETARY RIGHTS WHICH WE OWN.

WE GIVE YOU FORMAL NOTICE OF COPYRIGHT AND TRADEMARK INFRINGEMENT
AND UNFAIR COMPETITION. WE DEMAND THAT PRIOR TO THE CLOSE
OF BUSINESS SEPTEMBER 21, 1982 YOU ADVISE US IN WRITING AT
NIVERSAL CITY STUDIOS, INC., 100 UNIVERSAL CITY PLAZA,
UNIVERSAL CITY, CA 91608, OF THE FOLLOWING: (1) THAT YOU
HAVE CEASED ALL DISTRIBUTION AND SALE OF ANY E.T. MERCHANDISE;
(2) THAT YOU ADVISE US OF THE TOTAL NUMBER OF GOODS SOLD AND
THE TOTAL REVENUES RECEIVED; (3) THAT YOU ADVISE US OF ALL
MANUFACTURING SOURCES YOU HAVE USED; (4) THAT YOU INDICATE
YOUR WILLINGNESS TO SURRENDER ALL UNSOLD GOODS FOR DESTRUCTION
AND UNDERTAKE THAT YOU WILL NOT SELL OR DISTRIBUTE ANY OTHER
SUCH GOODS.

UPON RECEIPT OF THIS INFORMATION, WE WILL BE IN A POSITION
TO DISCUSS THE PAYMENT OF DAMAGES. IN THE EVENT WE DO
NOT HEAR FROM YOU WITHIN THE PERIOD OF TIME SET FORTH IN
THIS TELEGRAM, WE SHALL TAKE SUCH OTHER FURTHER AND SERIOUS
ACTION AS MAY BE APPROPRIATE TO PROTECT OUR INTERESTS.

THIS WIRE IS WITHOUT PREJUDICE TO OUR RIGHT TO ULTIMATELY
SEEK DAMAGES, INCLUDING PUNITIVE DAMAGES.

    UNIVERSAL CITY STUDIOS, INC.
    100 UNIVERSAL CITY PLAZA
    UNIVERSAL CITY, CA 91608
    BY: JOHN G. NUANES, ATTORNEY

TR

1734 EST

consciousness for quite some time. "Damages," "Payment" — they sound especially awesome. And they all sound like money, my money. What a dire threat, indeed, I seemed to be for the greatest Hollywood moneymaker of all time! By now, my own personal expenses in the project had exceeded $400, all loss — no profit.

So what might be my reaction? A lawyer fast! My high school chum, Jack Gibson, had become an attorney about the time I completed graduate school. I quickly drove to his office where I told him my plight. He responded with guffaws and immediately dictated a letter to California which must be presented at this time.

The somewhat choppy quality of Jack's dictated prose indicates the spontaneity of his response as well as the rapidity with which he decided to communicate with the studio. After all, I had been given something like six hours to tell Universal that, among other things, I had agreed to the destruction of my booklets. The thrill of "creation" had suddenly metamorphosed into icy fear that I really must have been in deep legal trouble.

But, of course, there was the tone of Jack Gibson's letter, especially seen in the conciliatory conclusion. He even tried a bit of southern hospitality to placate the powers that be. I was particularly interested in what sense of humor the "big boys" might have regarding my situation. The answers to my questions were and are never to be known, apparently. For as I said before, no other direct contact with me has ever occurred. "Negotiations" did take place, however, between the attorneys. Mr. Nuanes of Universal became the point of contact for Mr. Gibson. But before proceeding further, I must explain what really precipitated the entire incident.

As mentioned, I reluctantly attended *E.T.* when my three daughters, Valerie, Ginger, and Heather, begged to see the movie. This was in the early part of July 1982. On my first view-

# HOLLYWOOD AND THE PROFESSOR: THE FLEA'S REPRIEVE

**MASON, GIBSON AND COWARDIN**
ATTORNEYS AT LAW
893 J. CLYDE MORRIS BOULEVARD
NEWPORT NEWS, VIRGINIA 23601

SHANNON T. MASON, JR.
JONATHAN S. GIBSON, III
WILLIAM C. COWARDIN, JR.

DONALD L. MOORE
SPECIAL COUNSEL

ALFRED O. MASTERS, JR.

AREA CODE
(804)
595-7275

September 21, 1982

Mr. John G. Nuanes
Attorney at Law
Universal City Studios, Inc.
100 Universal City Plaza
Universal City, CA 91608

Re: Dr. Albert E. Millar, Jr.

Dear Mr. Nuanes:

    Dr. Millar is head of the English Department at our local college, Christopher Newport.

    He took his children to see "E.T." and although his interest centers on medieval literature and early american history, he was impressed by Mr. Spielberg's work.

    He prepared the enclosed brochure subsequent to his sending the letter dated July 26, 1982, a copy of which is enclosed.

    If you will note, he has made some 33 scripture parallels to "E.T.". Dr. Millar's father is a minister of long standing in this community.

    The picture of "E.T." was prepared by an 18 year old student at Christopher Newport College.

    Mr. Millar spent approximately three to four hundred dollars having the pamphlets printed. His original concept was to pay for his initial investment by charging a dollar for each pamphlet sold. To date he has received $23.00. I have told him not to sell any more of these brochures at this point.

    Dr. Millar really did not enter into this with a commercial intent in mind. His July 26, 1982 letter clarifies his intent.

## HOLLYWOOD AND THE PROFESSOR: THE FLEA'S REPRIEVE

As I stated previously, he sold 23 of these to date. He has distributed some of these pamphlets to his students in his Bible as literature class at the college.

You may not be aware of this, but there has been some resistance to the picture "E.T." by some of the fundamentalistic religious churches in the area. They claim that the picture is satanically inspired.

The gentleman who printed the approximately 200 copies of this pamphlet is a Mr. Sam Royall. Mr. Royall is the individual that Dr. Millar makes reference to in paragraph five of his letter.

The local newspaper was going to do a story on how Dr. Millar developed his interpretation of the movie "E.T.". I have asked them to cancel that until I can hear from you. I would suggest that there is a question of academic freedom in this matter. I think Dr. Millar was attempting to ascertain if he had permission for his endeavor with his July 26, 1982 letter.

I would think you would probably pick up close to an extra two or three hundred thousand dollars in movie revenues if the church communities in this area realized there was no satanic intent by Mr. Spielberg.

Can you imagine what would happen if I turn his July 26, 1982 letter, with your telegram, over to the newspaper? You could hear the laughter in California. I know you want to protect the $400,000,000.00 that the press indicates Mr. Spielberg's creation has generated; however, I don't think this is quite the serious matter which really requires the full force of the Federal Judiciary.

It would be nice if the community could benefit in some manner from Dr. Millar's religious interpretation of "E.T.". You can rest assure that no one is trying to infringe on "E.T.'s" copyright.

I think Spielberg Productions should fly Dr. Millar to California and put him on national television. There's a whole untapped market out there just waiting for the right blessing.

I am awaiting your instructions.

Virginia is lovely at this time of year. If you want anybody to investigate the matter, I would suggest that they arrive sometime before the middle of October so that they can enjoy the autumn foliage in the valley of Virginia.

Very truly yours,

Jonathan S. Gibson, III

JSG,III:met
enc.

ing, I almost instantly recognized 24 parallels that seem to exist between E.T. and Jesus. In a state of near disbelief over what just couldn't have been a collection of coincidences, I surprised my family less than a week later with an invitation to return to the movie a second time. They, of course, accepted with delight another opportunity to enjoy the whole experience once again. Vickie, my wife, and I, with our three girls, waited until the next "bargain" day at the Riverdale Theater.

I had a specific intent on my second viewing of *E.T.* I knew the audience was (and is) primarily motivated by the entertainment afforded by this most significant summer classic. That factor, for me, was not important at this time for I had taken into the darkened theater my pen and a large envelope. So supplied, I wanted to record what other parallels might be present in the movie. I planned to catch any new details pertaining to the religious basis I had discovered in the first showing a few days earlier. Even while writing my responses almost illegibly in the dark, I was not disappointed. Not in the slightest.

When I emerged into the afternoon heat after participating in the applause that seems to be a fixture at the conclusion of every showing of *E.T.*, I checked my scribbled-over envelope to find that I had detected nine more items which showed similarities between E.T. and Jesus. Almost feverishly, I combined them with my preceding 24 to complete the total. I then wrote a kind of prose poem and a brief essay to serve as an introduction to the list of 33 parallels.

My essential motivation at the time was to share with others what many people told me they could "see" once someone pointed it out to them. And this was the concept that Christian parable was inherent in the script of *E.T.* I believed that it was intentional. I believed that the positive response on the part of millions of moviegoers had a basis that was somewhat deeper than mere entertainment over a robotic cutie's problems in what for him was certainly an alien society. I felt so strongly that others ought to know these things that I quickly polished my notes and took them to the Williamsburg Press where my good friend, Sam Royall, works for his father, the owner.

Sam noticed my eagerness to see what I had written go into print and said he would handle the job as quickly as his schedule permitted. At that particular time, I was concluding a busy schedule of teaching summer school at my college, Christopher Newport in Newport News. I was also about to take the family to Disney World for a vacation. So, I left my manuscript, including a sketch of E.T. drawn by RH Wallace, one of my favorite students, in Sam's capable hands. And my next few days were spent with Dumbo, Mickey, Space Mountain, and the expansive sands of Daytona Beach. But my attention remained riveted on E.T. His influence continued to be pervasive in spite of a change in scenery. My time in Florida was largely one of distraction, but pleasant, nonetheless.

Upon returning home, I was pleased to find in my mailbox a few advance copies of *"E.T."—You're More Than a Movie Star*. Sam Royall had expertly printed my entire pamphlet and had arranged everything neatly on four and a half pages. It was now approaching the last week of July. At this time, the movie was setting box office records everywhere. The media began mentioning the multiple millions it was earning for Mr. Spielberg and for Universal.

Yet very few people seemed to have any awareness of my particular interpretation of one reason why the movie grips them the way it does. And I was still very anxious to show them what I had written. How to do this remained a major problem. Could I advertise? Could I meet my expenses? Should I tell the studio what I had done? Should I request permission, albeit after the fact of printing the booklet? Thoughts such as these continued to crop up, but I really saw nothing insurmountable at the time.

On July 26, 1982, I wrote directly to Steven Spielberg in care of Universal Studios explaining precisely what I was doing regarding their creation. As the letter indicates, I felt that nothing but praise should be rendered to those responsible for giving us a "good" movie, an experience in sharing and feeling that seemed to transcend the capacity of celluloid. Exactly as the letter was written, I present it here:

July 26, 1982

Mr. Steven Spielberg
c/o MCA—Universal Studios
Hollywood, CA 90028

Dear Mr. Spielberg:

    I first wanted to offer my thanks to you for giving us E.T. My family hasn't been moved by anything like this in many years. It is a well-deserved success.
    But the primary reason for my writing to you is to offer you the first copy of my booklet giving my own reaction to the remarkable number of parallels that seem to exist between your brilliantly conceived little character and Jesus. I simply couldn't believe the obvious comparisons and so I wrote them down for a few of my friends to see. One of my friends is a printer in Williamsburg, and he asked me if he could print the thoughts in booklet form along with a sketch of E.T. drawn by a young student of mine at Christopher Newport College. The result is enclosed.
    I have no idea whether my own interpretation differs from what your intentions may have been. And I certainly don't intend to offend anyone by stating my ideas.
    What I really must say is that I feel the need to ask you whether I need permission to present these concepts of the movie and whether I ought to remove the sketch from the cover. I am perfectly willing to abide by whatever you and the studio deem proper.

I have been teaching the Bible as literature for years, and I am perhaps more prone to "see" Biblical parallels than most people. Regardless, I must tell you that one devout Christian who saw my booklet said he thanked God for it because he feared that there was a "demonic" influence in the movie. He now, much to his delight, is allowing his children to see the movie.

I plan to advertise the little booklet in a few newspapers and to charge $1.00 per copy. This ought to cover the printing, handling, and mailing costs. By no means could I profit from this. I just feel that people may like to have another way of understanding E.T.

I would really enjoy hearing from you any comments you may wish to make regarding *"E.T."—You're More Than a Movie Star.*

Sincerely yours,
Albert E. Millar, Jr., Ph.D.
Professor and Chairman of English


I have no clue where this letter ended up, or who might have seen it, and there certainly was no reply. My opinion is that it might be housed with the thousands of fan letters that Mr. Spielberg must be receiving regarding the phenomenon he created with *E.T.* My epistolary connection with him truly seems to be Gone with the Wind.

As the weeks passed since mailing the letter, I still pursued the idea of spreading my interpretation as widely as possible. My wishes to do this were confirmed by very positive reactions on the part of friends and family members who read the pamphlet. Since I continued to hear nothing from the studio one way or the other, I yielded to frustration by placing an ad in *The New York Times*. This maneuver netted me no replies. Undaunted, I placed another ad with (of all things) the *National Enquirer*. Results? I received 23 requests for copies of the booklet. This was not quite my idea of successfully "reaching" potential interested readers.

Still there was no word from Hollywood, or anywhere else for that matter.

When the Public Relations director of Christopher Newport College, Paula Delo, saw my booklet, she called the local press. Hence, there was a newspaper story about how I came to write about E.T. and Jesus. But that was the extent of the entire episode until the studio reacted so vociferously in late September when the now infamous telegram arrived. When the Associated Press received word of all that ensued on September 26, 1982, the results were astounding. My story, the *Studio vs. the Professor, Money vs. the Lord, or David and Goliath,* was printed all over the continent and through *Stars and Stripes,* in Europe and the Orient. Very quickly, it now seems, everyone heard I had produced a booklet. And the interest of the people was geared toward the legal aspect of what I had done, not really toward the spiritual dimension which I saw in the movie. But at least they were hearing something, even though I seemed to be cast in an increasingly negative role.

An article that appeared in *The Washington Post* the next day typifies the type of publicity I was receiving. And free of charge, I might add:

## "E.T. and Jesus: Virginia Professor Warned to Drop Booklet Comparing Them"

NEWPORT NEWS, Sept. 26 (AP) – Universal City Studios has warned a Virginia college professor against continuing to distribute a pamphlet he produced comparing the movie, *E.T. the Extra-Terrestrial* with the life of Jesus. Universal City Studios attorney John G. Nuanes notified Albert E. Millar, Jr., chairman of the English Department at Christopher Newport College here, that sales of the booklet "without our consent ... infringe upon the proprietary rights which we own." Nuanes asked that the professor advise the studio he has "ceased all distribution and sale of any E.T. merchandise"; that he advise them of the number of copies and all revenues; and that he "advise us of all manufacturing sources."

"It's like using an atomic bomb to kill a flea," said Millar of the studio's telegram.

In his pamphlet, Millar, who teaches a course on the Bible as literature, listed 33 items in the movie he believes closely parallel the life of Jesus. He published the booklet titled, *"E.T."—You're More than a Move Star* in July at his own expense. He then wrote the movie's creator, Steven Spielberg, explaining his reasons and sent Spielberg, a copy of the pamphlet. He has sold 23 of the booklets.

———

By being a "troublemaker" or a perceived threat to the rights the studio held, I became "known." This was not exactly as I, or anyone, might have wished to have such a thing happen; but my concept of the movie could be shared nonetheless, even in this unusual fashion. Many people now seemed to want to read my piece on E.T. Perhaps they did so because the studio's actions seemed to remove the possibility that the pamphlet would even exist for long. The old saying that deprivation enhances need seemed especially appropriate now.

## CHAPTER TWO
## "Somebody Noticed"

Perhaps without catching German measles in the second grade, I'd be able to write my name clearly enough to be legible. For handwriting has remained a problem for me in spite of attendance at five universities throughout my academic career. I've always thought that my absenteeism at age seven from Hilton School surely must have contributed in some frightful way to the scrawl that I've had to call my own since the late 1940s. It must be either that excuse or another in the neighborhood of sloth.

This has at no time been truer than now. For as I speak at civic groups, conventions, and churches, I've been asked by very nice people to autograph copies of my "E.T booklet." How I wish the recipients of those "tokens" could hide their crestfallen looks when they try to read the message scratched across the page. I've even been asked to "translate" for some of the more courageous autograph-seekers. And one young lady at a meeting of the National Association of Government Secretaries actually asked me to do hers over. And quite obviously I had to agree with her. The problem is that the fresher writing produced no less satisfactory results than the original. But such is the price, I'm learning quickly enough, of that most ephemeral state of the human condition — fame.

For in all the years of teaching college English, the only marks I made on others' papers have been in red ink. And they have struck more fear than appreciation for their receivers, I'm sure. So why do some people seem to beam with pride when I write a cryptic message to them on the little booklets I wrote in July 1982? Why, for instance, do they wait patiently in line several dozen deep to have me write a message to their grandchildren carrying their own names? Or why might they abandon their own reserve to ask, even bluntly, if I would sign just my name, as clearly as I might manage on a 5-1/2 by 8-1/2 paper which forms the inside of the cover to *"E.T."—You're More Than a Movie Star?* My introduction to being "famous" was completely unexpected and as sudden as anything I've ever experienced or heard about from anyone else.

The Sunday morning the *Daily Press* carried my story brought a television crew from the local ABC affiliate (WVEC) into my living room, countless phone calls from radio stations seeking comments, and even a clarifying interview from the Associated Press. And in the early afternoon of the same day, I received a call from a former student, the Reverend Jack Hundley, who told me he was driving through Pennsylvania and heard on his car radio about my circumstances on ABC national news. Others reported hearing about me on the Turner Cable News Network that evening. Local news shows were beginning to speak of the "celebrity" professor before the day's end. The events of that day were terminated near midnight by a reporter's phone call from Norfolk, Virginia, who wanted to do a front-page story on me for the *Ledger-Star.*

And the very next day, I returned to teaching but found my powers of concentration to be ebbing as I fielded among others calls from the International Media Services as well as *Saturday Night Live.* I also accepted two opportunities to be on live talk shows in San Francisco on KGO with Jim Eason and on KGNR in Sacramento with Jack Kirkwood. My mail also was proving to be somewhat more interesting than before. In fact, I never received much of anything of note in my college mailbox prior to the instant notoriety that comes from being a "child of the media."

On the third day, I was discussed on national television on *Entertainment Tonight* (September 28, 1982) and appeared on KZZO by phone in Salt Lake City. Within twenty-four hours, I was interviewed on KCBS and KMEL in California and went on an hour-long call-in show with Allan Dale on WOAI in San Antonio, Texas. Needless to say, my life was dramatically changing, and I was yet to determine if this was for the better. After all, thoughts of Universal's displeasure with me diminished any real sense of accomplishment I felt over being able to communicate my views with increasingly large numbers of listeners. The "trouble" I was in seemed to widen the potential forum, however.

That "trouble" was to hit home rather quickly and literally. Having teenaged daughters, I encountered their displeasure for the first time over Daddy's use of the phone. Who, indeed, had ever wanted to talk to him? Now, it seemed, the world wished for "Dr. E.T." to comment on how, in heaven's name, he could have seen those things about Jesus in a mere movie. And to compound the disbelief of my interviewers, I had to reiterate that my total involvement with the movie was two viewings separated by about a week. Countless times, I recited how I felt almost compelled to organize my thoughts in print to share my findings with as many people as possible. Of course, my children hoped that I would find a means to do so that would not interfere with their primary social outlet—talking on the phone! Alas, for a time this was just not to be.

Neighbors who had barely noticed I lived near them began waving as at a long-lost friend as they passed me on the street next to my home. Some rather sheepishly asked for a copy of the booklet to "show the preacher." Others decided that it was time to have a chat with me about where their offspring might attend college down the line. To parents of kindergartners, this kind of information seemed to be just a bit premature. But I found by being available and by remaining as friendly as possible, I was not hurting my cause. And, besides, I really had always hoped for a warmer spirit of neighborliness anyway, wherever I might happen to be. I had to register this as a large "plus" regarding these particular developments concerning my becoming better known than before.

I suppose the only real hardship on the homefront was that endured by my wife, Vickie, who had to scurry about with some pretty energetic housekeeping since there would be surprise visitors nowadays. She was especially anxious for the living room to look as neat as possible since the earliest of several television interviews were done there. All in all, she seemed fascinated by the new attention her middle-aged husband was now receiving and weathered the change in our lifestyles most admirably. And through all the events of my "public" life, not one person who visited us mentioned dust or clutter. This is even more remarkable since our household includes a normal six-year-old and a minor panther of a cat.

Yet of all those who reacted to my changed status, no group has registered more responsiveness than those who are around me more often than anybody—my students. My captive audiences for the Fall 1982 semester had front row seats for the drama of their English professor's dilemma and were privy to all developing events. They were exuberant; they were quizzical; they were definitely showing more interest in this than they had ever shown in the *Harbrace Handbook* or George Orwell. An evident dividend also included an upswing in attendance. They didn't seem to want to miss any details in the new life of what many said was the only celebrity they had ever known.

All of this was especially pertinent to my English 300 course on the Bible as literature. The essential approach I had always made in that class was to have the students see what possible ways the Scriptures could be viewed as literature. We discussed poetic, biographical, fictive, elegiac, historical, and prophetic concepts each Wednesday night as we perused the Dartmouth Bible together. How fortuitous, it seemed, that people were beginning to notice that there could be a Biblical kind of parallel presented through the vehicle of cinematic entertainment! Each student received gratis a copy of my booklet and an invitation to consider his or her own response to the movie whenever viewing it might be possible. (All the while, I kept wondering whether Universal might appreciate all the advertising the company might be receiving through my difficulties—a point some individuals have suggested could have been engineered from the beginning.)

Two student responses to my newfound "fame" really need mention. One high school student reported to me that while he was strolling the halls of his school, he saw an attractive sophomore opening her locker door to reveal a newspaper picture of me neatly clipped and taped within. I honestly don't think Tom Selleck had a thing to worry about here! But I suppose becoming a pin-up at any stage of life is a novelty to be remembered.

The other significant reaction came from within one of my freshman English sections. Just after warning my students about the pitfalls of comma splices, I assigned an essay on the ugliest or the most beautiful thing they could recall seeing. One might imagine my surprise to read the topic selected by an especially perky seventeen-year-old, her own English class as a beautiful place. This was a definite first, and probably the unlikeliest choice of "beauty" I had ever encountered. But as I present her completed product here, I believe we must agree that a particularly personal interest in my (in her eyes) increased stature strongly influenced her choice of topic. Everyone must be allowed to dream, of course. But somehow could not envisage my English 101 class as another Schwab's drug store. Nonetheless, Jennifer's essay goes as follows:

### The Most Beautiful Place - My English 101 Class

In my opinion, the most beautiful place is my English 101 classroom. This feeling derives from the joyous and entertaining moments I have spent there. My professor, Doctor Albert Millar, is the main reason for this, for he is entertainment himself.

Twice a week, thirty or so of us students sit enthralled as Doctor Millar teaches us what we have found can be fun—English! Doctor Millar's controversial pamphlet *"E.T." — You're More Than Movie Star*, has made a popular subject on campus, in class, and around the nation.

I find this pamphlet as the break I have been waiting for all my life; it is my chance at stardom! As the media swarm the campus, I will make myself readily available as a guide to them. I plan, as I'm showing the press Doctor Millar's parking space and classroom, to get on film at crucial moments. Then, hopefully, an aspiring director or producer will see me and realize my true star quality. Even if I do not become a nationally known celebrity, Doctor Millar's students are so popular on campus because E.T. is hotter gossip than what Luke is up to on General Hospital, and I am sure to get to know many important people that way.

When I entered college, I thought it would be a hard four years of work before I could make my mark on the world. With the help of E.T. I'm hopeful that stardom will come sooner. If so, then I will not wait all the time in college while I could be the newest sex symbol.

I admire her spunk, anyway.

In yet another class, my survey of early English literature, the students had an opportunity to share in the "media blitz" that was occurring in early October 1982. When a camera crew came to photograph me opening stacks of mail in my campus office for the evening news, I had to retreat to the classroom for a noon-hour class. Without hesitation, the reporter and her cameraman followed me, lights and all, down the hall and into the room where 36 students waited for my lecture on Spenser's *Faerie Queene* to begin. As the camera rolled, I stood behind the lectern discussing the multiple allegories Spenser concocted for his masterpiece. And the students, especially those within range of the videotape, primped and checked their hair so they could beam their way into the hearts of America. My brother called a few days later to say he saw the interview, including my students, on Channel 5 in Los Angeles!

One of my brightest English majors, Melissa Huffman, was interviewed alone in my office to comment on the students' reaction that was happening to her professor. Her televised comment that I had not been "changed" by the events of recent weeks was somewhat reassuring. She had indicated, however, that she felt I was "deep down" bothered somewhat by what had happened to me. Without showing any real concern over the deeper meaning of the student interview, I continued to chair my department and teach my four classes as well as possible. Unquestionably, everything I did seemed to be somehow different than before. Possibly the ways in which others perceived me contributed to this feeling.

As a kind of bridge between my settled, tenured existence in prior years and my increasingly turbulent time in the post-pamphlet era, one of the earliest letters I received from among hundreds that came in during that first week was from a former student. Kathy had remained a pleasant memory in the decade or so since she graduated [and] I found her insights to be especially noteworthy for the perspective she brought to bear. I also deeply appreciated hearing of her success in a market that seemed increasingly difficult for the survival of the liberal arts major. She had written on the very day my story was originally circulated.

The combination of Kathy's comments and those of many, many others was beginning to assist me in dealing with the depression I was entering over the troubles I might have contracted for myself because of E.T. People really seemed to care who I was and what I had done. Notice this analysis done of me a whole continent away on the next day:

9-27-82

Hi! Please send one E.T. booklet to the address below. Enclosed is $1.40 to help the cost of the stamp and envelope. It was nice to hear you on K.G.N.R. radio and you sound like a nice, thoughtful person. I'm glad that an observant person is sharing an observation. I'm also glad that there is a soul in the world that views things from a biblical perspective.

Keep up the good work — and thanks!!

L. Schooler (California)

---

And from Nebraska on the same day came this response:

9-27-82

Thank you for making the news! Being a scholar of the Bible will bring even more attention than would otherwise be possible! Jesus Christ will win overall! I am not a scholar but am a follower, believer of Jesus Christ ... A CHRISTIAN! The similarities between the "potato head" and my Savior were glaring to me! It is very interesting to see how few see the connection! Jesus Christ, not a registered trademark, His life story, not copyrighted, certainly is open to misuse, unlike the creature. Personally, I would like to have a copy of your exposé, if possible. If not keep the money for your expenses. Thanks for the courage and effort.

Sincerely,
L. K. (Nebraska)

———

I noticed with increasingly keen interest how the legal aspects of my "case" were being handled by certain individuals. But I must return now to the birth of my fame, fleetingly arriving, and equally so in its departure.

Calls and letters continued very briskly for the first few weeks. I was especially interested to hear from people in Canada, Puerto Rico, and even Israel. I remain in awe over the effectiveness of the media. For reasons that are not completely clear, I seemed to have been more newsworthy than I deserved to be. Many major newspapers used my story on their front pages, as a matter of fact. *The Los Angeles Time*s placed me higher in their "Newsmakers" section than Princess Stephanie and the Pope!

I later learned of accounts written about me in several Sunday magazines and weekly newspapers throughout the nation. Several readers would clip out different stories about the "E.T. Professor" and include them in their letters to me. At my family's suggestion, I began placing these clippings in a large file rather quickly. Something here for the grandchildren, I suppose.

Through my workdays, I would continue to wonder about what could happen next. All of the events surrounding my "discovery" by the larger world beyond Tidewater, Virginia, had been without rhyme or reason. The unpredictable nature of the events transpiring became a constant factor. As the first month continued to pass, I would find at the conclusion of teaching a class my secretary, Mary, waiting in the hall with messages I might have missed. One day she said, "*Newsweek* called." On another, she brought me a phone number from a man named Smith who said he had lined up television and guest speaking engagements in Washington, D.C. Interestingly, he never delivered what he had promised. Everything in balance, I had to say.

Another caller from California said, "We will publish anything you've written. "Oh, how tempting some of these mysterious parties were to me—probably the best known "unpublished" author in America.

Stranger and stranger responses were looming. For instance, I received reams of materials from a UFO organization in California demonstrating to me that, yes, extraterrestrials are very much present in our lives. I was amazed at what possible association they were assigning to me of their beliefs. Had I been declared an "expert" in the unusual? I'm simply attempting to present samples of the communications I was receiving as a result of Universal's actions. For certain, there was an amazing diversity to the letters I was continuing to find whenever I visited my mailbox.

But the ultimate in being known was still ahead of me. I had accepted many regional speaking engagements and did a few more television talk-shows on the local channels and was kept immensely busy trying to send out pamphlets to those who continued to request them. In this way, I was passing the second month of my E.T. notoriety. I even began to sense that interest may be ebbing as I fully expected it would.

But on November 16, I found that I had not exactly resumed anonymity. A special correspondent for *People Weekly*, Doris Bacon, phoned me twice from her office in Beverly Hills, California. She asked me several questions about my booklet, the publicity I had received, and the course I teach in the Bible as literature. She also requested that I mail her any pertinent information I had on E.T. and me. These I quickly sent as I had a taping for a television show that afternoon and a conference address to deliver that evening.

Three days later, I received a call from Mr. Tom Brook of BBC-TV who wanted me to come to the New York studio of their network to be taped for a program to be shown in England called *Nationwide*. On November 23, I went to New York at Mr. Brook's invitation to tape a segment of a program that would introduce *E.T.* to the English people. I discussed some of the movie's highlights, my booklet and its contents, and showed several *E.T.* products that were flooding the American market. I had positively looted my children's rooms of E.T. tennis shoes, shoelace's, dolls, tee shirts, drinking glasses, posters, bubble gum cards, and even the record of the movie's theme music. I also took with me my six-year-old Heather's E.T. Halloween costume. Mr. Brook, who seemed to be enjoying my "obsession" with all of this, requested that I do part of the interview wearing the E.T. mask I had managed to slip out of the house for my trip. While gazing at the camera high above Rockefeller Center, I wondered behind the mask of E.T.'s face whether anyone who knew me would see me in this less than dignified role.

A former student named Karen Weckhorst happened to be tuned in to BBC-1 on the evening of December 10 when the program aired. The network timed the program to coincide with the premiere in London of *E.T.,* which was attended by Prince Charles and Princess Diana. Karen's letter indicated that she never knew that her English professor was an "international TV star." I can assure her that he isn't, but I found the entire experience to be exhilarating. My venture into being "famous" seemed to be approaching real proportions. Could I be involved in something more than a game after all? But I guess it is too soon (and maybe always is) to find meaning in the manifold events of our lives.

It was during the 1982 Christmas season that I was to receive the widest exposure I would ever know. For in the special double issue of *People* magazine dated December 27 — January 3, 1983, there I was on page 69 describing reactions to the phenomenon of *E.T.* The article spelled my name correctly, referred to my college, gave the title of the pamphlet, and also cited two of my 33 parallels. And even more fascinating to me was the estimate on the part of *People's* editors that this special year-end edition would have 43 million readers!

My emotions were more spirited than at any time since I first saw the movie. My goal of telling people what I thought about a very special experience with a popular movie was now fully realized. But wait—wasn't I being sued or something?

E.T.

SHORT ON LOOKS (BUT NOT LOVING FANS), AN ALIEN FINDS HIS HOME IN HOLLYWOOD

eventually speaks to the alienated soul deep within us all.
For some, like English professor Albert Millar Jr., 41, of Christopher Newport College in Virginia, the movie is a quasi-religious parable. Citing E.T.'s resurrection, his powers of healing and 31 other points, Millar has published a pamphlet, titled *E.T.—You're More Than a Movie Star*, comparing the alien's adventures to the story of Christ. For others, especially the mil-

## CHAPTER THREE
## A More Famous "Flea"

All through my experiences with the media and with individuals who commented to me about what I had done with *E.T.*, I noticed that the most significant issue remained—Universal's telegram and its potential consequences. Nothing else seemed as remotely interesting to them as how it felt to be on the hot seat of a major entertainment company such as MCA-Universal. No one, absolutely no one, seemed to believe me when I tried to reply to questions on the subject of being sued that I admired the company that gave us *E.T.*

I truly remained awestruck by the underlying message of the movie and knew that without the production facilities and almost limitless resources for research in special effects, none of us would have met the most charming little character to have come our way in years. For some inexplicable reason, I couldn't bring myself to become overly concerned about what this seemingly faceless company could do to an individual who had attempted to explain their own success. Maybe I was displaying the epitome of naivete.

I kept telling myself in those early days of my "infamy" that I had my own fairly straight life-record to rely on. I also knew that the studio couldn't have the complete facts on what I had written or, indeed, what my intentions might have been. Indubitably, I knew they would have to agree that I had no capacity whatsoever to siphon off any measurable profits from either the movie or its concomitant products that were soon to be as available as a horde of locusts in Moses' Egypt. What reassured me after receipt of that telegram was the blithe feeling that once the legals of Universal got to know me, they might even congratulate me on my perception of their artistic endeavor. Violating copyright protection just wasn't a part of it, so I continued to say in increasingly more frequent silent prayers. But the fact remained that I had done something to deserve their notice and more. I had technically without their consent analyzed their product and to avoid bankruptcy tried to charge others a dollar each to send them my writing. I guess there were times when I could see things in a more "universal" way. Maybe I was guilty of what they said in spite of my previously stated intentions. I was haunted by ambiguity. I could see "rights" on both sides.

Another comfort I took in the early going was the copy of the letter I had mailed to Mr. Spielberg in care of the studio on July 26. I also had to recall that if I had waited for a reply, I'd still be doing so. And many people wouldn't have known the Christian parallels that imbued the movie. So, my "guilt" seemed to be haste. But as I said, I did wait close to two months. Couldn't these factors be viable considerations if I might be allowed to present my side? Of course, by this time I felt that even foreknowledge of the "threat" would not have been sufficient to stifle my expression of thoughts. The source of such courage I still can't ascertain. Probably an alternative label for me would be lunacy, as at least some could suggest. In fact, during the interview I did for BBC-TV, I recalled Mr. Brook saying, "How do you deal with people who might think you're 'crackers?'" No satisfactory answer surfaced, unfortunately. (I knew I shouldn't have worn that E.T. mask!)

One of the early newspaper accounts of my problem with Universal said that the initials "E.T." represented the words "Extra Trouble" for a certain professor, me. Some room is always allowed for "cute," especially if it is at the expense of another. Or, indeed, if it might inspire the purchase of an extra paper or two, some people don't mind a bit what mileage could be obtained from the difficulties of another. Overall, however, the accounts I was able to read presented the facts as well as possible. My difficulty was, of course, that the facts were so visible thanks to the interest so many portions of the media had taken in my story.

Because of the outreaching effects that seemed tentacle-like, to be affecting those many people who were aware of me by now, I started filing away several key letters that commented on the "threat" against me. Many of these responses carried the most sincere tones of caring for the "little man" who had exercised his First Amendment prerogative. And a few individuals even suggested that they took pride in me for "speaking forth" on my beliefs. One caller even said he had encouraged his organization, Christian Legal, to phone Universal Studios every hour to protest their hardheaded treatment of that "Professor." As a sample of the earlier responses to my being ordered to cease distribution of the pamphlets, I include few of the most pertinent letters I was receiving in the first week or so.

The first had a most impressive letterhead, the Academy of Motion Picture Arts and Sciences. Mrs. Carol Epstein of the Academy's Margaret Herrick Library wrote to request a copy of my "E.T. piece" for their files. (I suppose I have become a tiny part of Hollywood history by now.) She also said in regard to my "flap" with Universal that she was on my side. She also said, "Let's see more serious writing on E.T."

Another letter spoke most knowledgeably of my situation because it came from "within the family," or at least formerly so.

Yet another person wrote after reading of me in the *Los Angeles Times* to say that, if anything, "God should be suing Universal Studios for copyright infringement because E.T. imitated Christ in 33 instances." The writer then went on to offer his support in my struggle with the studio. I was more and more encouraged with the daily arrival of several more similar statements from people who demonstrated their concern for me.

One person simply said to me, "Look! They've already gotten in trouble for copying the Sistine Chapel ceiling for their touching-finger ads. What have you got to worry about?" The only problem with that is Michelangelo can't be sent a telegram. Or at least he can't receive one. Another said quite simply: "Good luck with your injunction, suit, or whatever with Universal Studios. You actually are creating an even greater interest in *E.T.* Too bad Universal Studios can't see this." I really wonder if they did.

Probably the most memorable response to the warning I received occurred on the Christopher Newport campus when members of the student body started what they called the "E.T. Defense Fund" and posted it on a colleague's door. They relished their anonymity and wrote "pledges" on the sheet that ranged from a free plastic surgery consultation to an offer of rights to the sequel of *E.T.* called *E.T.C.* One I particularly liked as a Bible teacher was the contribution that included an "active harem." This one actually wasn't far removed from the atmosphere of Old Testament studies!

As the list of items grew over the following months, it boasted several bizarre items that were intended to "help Dr. Millar through his trial against Universal." What worried me, though, was the label for the sheet listing the offers. It claimed "Defense" for E.T. At the time, E.T. was doing very well, very well indeed. He obviously needed no defense at all. It was I who seemed very much to need defending.

In the next few weeks after receiving news that I had offended a major company, I was deeply touched by the kindness extended to me by many students at my college, many of whom had never actually been in my classes. They said things like, "We're with you," or "We'll picket the courthouse when they try you and then the jail when they convict you." I felt a mixed blessing by their emotional outbursts.

Also, the school newspaper was having a field day with me. I was photographed on the front page in an apparent rage under an article called, "Dr. Millar, You're More Than an English Professor." Actually, I think I was only making an especially strong point about writing fragments on formal freshman essays. *The Captain's Log* included a multi-columned interview I had given a school reporter where I tried to state my side as succinctly and objectively as possible. I repeated my view that I was continuing to act with no malice or harshness toward Mr. Spielberg or the studio that owned *E.T.* and its spin-offs. I was actually beginning to suspect that some of my interviewers were attempting to goad me to exacerbate the situation. While being interviewed for a live newscast on KCBS in San Francisco, I recalled a voice saying to me that I couldn't possibly have the means to "fight" the entire legal arm of Universal Studios. I quickly agreed. It was, and is, impossible to consider. I've always been a very passive type anyway. I always preferred to allow events, within reason, to sweep me along. After all, how many three-year tenderfoots (tenderfeet?) can you recall in the Boy Scouts of America? I may hold the record.

While I was still wondering what my future might hold, I knew that one person on campus really ought to be consulted — the college president. When I arrived in Dr. Jack Anderson's office, I felt a touch of regret that I had become involved in controversy. I felt that I had somehow tarnished myself in the eyes of the college administration. But as I approached the president's desk in his suite overlooking our Shoe Lane campus, I was puzzled by the expression on his face. "Al," he said, wearing the biggest grin I had ever thought possible of him, "I have one request of you, spell the name of the college right. People are going to know where we are because of you." Somehow stunned, I recovered enough presence of mind to recall that, as Christopher Newport College is the youngest four-year college in Virginia, there really were people, probably even in Newport News, who didn't know our location. So infamy pays too, I began to think. Being notorious does seem to have the oddest effects on one's associates.

Among the most pleasant aspects I encountered during all that took place after making the news was the visit to my campus office of one of my senior English majors. C. Colbert had been one of the students who observed the filming of my teaching Spenser and had, apparently, thought that her English professor needed more than verbal support. As I sat at my desk marking up yet another batch of freshman essays, here came this lovely brunette with misty eyes pressing into my hand an envelope with money for my "legal costs." I was so overwhelmed by her offer that I couldn't think of a suitable reply for several seconds.

Our college has a higher student age than most (27 or 28) and includes 87% working people. So in a non-affluent student body, for me to be given money was just about the most incredible effect I would encounter. I was so touched by this young lady's gesture that all I could do was mumble my thanks, ask her to keep the money until things got "really bad" for me, and pretend that I was overcome by a sudden attack of "contactitis." My, those floating dust particles in a musty college office are prevalent and a real hazard to one's comfort. I felt that I really must have uncovered a more genuine spirit of beneficence than in my generally pessimistic state could have ever otherwise recognized. Miss Colbert's words, "I just wanted to help," remain with me yet. How jaded we tend to be until we meet the exception to the norm.

My upward mood swing continued during the several speaking engagements I had begun to accept. I noticed that the various groups who asked me to speak wanted to know how I stood with Universal. They asked me as well what Steven Spielberg had said about my booklet or about what his opinion was concerning the "lawsuit." Of course, I had no answers to their questions since no contact with me was ever made. It was the general tone of the several groups that especially interested me, whether I was speaking to a church youth group or a science fiction convention. I could detect real concern for what might happen to me in the demeanor and in the comments of each group.

I really wasn't depicting the studio as the villain, but I found that, for the most part, the loyalties of my listeners remained with me. I was especially grateful to a Kiwanis group for giving me a standing ovation support after I had explained to them my position on the matter of the threat against my publication. As I extended to an increasingly larger audience information on my procedures, I found that almost nobody seemed to feel that anyone could make a very strong case against me. Encouragement under duress is a real cordial, and I was receiving healthy doses from many mysterious sources. The most poignant came by phone on October 1, 1982.

While enjoying a rare moment of quiet in my office on that Friday near the conclusion of the most tumultuous week I had ever experienced, I answered my phone to speak with a Mr. Ken Berger of North Lauderdale, Florida. He told me that he had read of me in his local newspaper and had heard me being discussed on *Entertainment Tonight*. He checked in local libraries there for the phone number of the English department at CNC. And finally, he seemed almost surprised that he actually reached me. I told him that I was glad his efforts to communicate with me were successful because his voice revealed that he was determined to tell me something of earnest importance. And so he did.

Mr. Berger related to me that his son had been stricken with leukemia and prior to his death at the age of five in July 1982, had requested that his parents take him to see *E.T.* Even though the child was so ill he had to be propped up in his seat in the theater, he watched the movie in rapt admiration. When it was over, he told his parents that he saw Jesus in the movie. "But Tony," his father said, "it was just a little creature." "No," Tony replied, "I saw Jesus in the movie."

And on a return visit to see *E.T.* even closer to Tony's death, he persisted in telling the Bergers that he saw Jesus in the movie. But his parents remained unaware of their son's "vision" through the tragic loss that too soon occurred. They discussed in the days that followed why Tony had said what he did when he was taken to see *E.T.*

It was only through hearing about my troubles with Universal that the media afforded Ken Berger an opportunity to find someone to help unravel the mystery of his son's insight. When he said to me on that day, "I understand because of you what Tony meant," I knew that I had accomplished more than I could have imagined in my pamphlet. I felt then that the legal trouble no longer really mattered.

Our two voices choking with emotion, Mr. Berger and I concluded the phone conversation with a promise on his part that he would help me any way he could. He said that I had brought peace to him and his wife since they now knew how to interpret the last words of their departed Tony. I promised to send the family one of my pamphlets and have continued to pray for their welfare. Nothing could have made my efforts more worthwhile, more real, than what I learned from the phone call of Ken Berger. To have received a legal scare back in September now seemed irrelevant.

In fact, I continue believing that the action of Universal City Studios requesting that I "cease and desist" from distributing the pamphlet was just the catalyst I had needed to extend my interpretation. It really is no wonder that I was beginning to feel a great deal more confident about the outcome. I had faith in the rightness, though perhaps not the timing, of my statements to share with others. For the sake of many people, especially the Bergers, I am very glad things happened the way they did.

## CHAPTER FOUR
## Reprieve?

Anyone who has been near a retail outlet recently has had to notice the *E.T.*-related paraphernalia that is available to the American (and now worldwide) public. As cute as some of the items are, one must wonder what people's saturation threshold might be, however. I have heard that some individuals need to "draw the line" on that lighted E.T. finger which has now appeared. But most buyers during the Christmas buying season of '82 seem to have been genuinely charmed by everything associated with this uncannily successful movie. Certain products such as the talking E.T. were almost impossible to keep stocked for Christmas shoppers as the year closed. Stories abounded about the profits many companies were deriving from their licensed right to fill the needs of affected buyers. On the tiniest E.T. erasures, or on the E.T. bicycle ($74), the imprint of Universal's copyright could be found. But this was not the case for all of the items.

Very early on when the phenomenal success of *E.T.* became known, many spokesmen started warning the public and perhaps even the company itself about "pirated" *E.T.* items. It seemed that a war was on to see who could grab the most lucrative share of an eager group of purchasers. Thus, many entrepreneurs were skirting completely around the envelope of copyright and trademark protection that Universal had established for the majority of items fostered by their remarkably popular vehicle.

Recently, my children received a little plastic representation of E.T. that convinced me MCA-Universal should be more fully protected by the laws of the land. At least the hope is that quality could be maintained by the procedures contributing to gaining the right to be legal. This gift to my children deservedly seemed to have had absolutely no chance of gaining legitimacy. It consisted of a smallish brown plastic form that purported to be E.T. Its eyes were blue enough, but the even more misshapen head could have fooled even the alien's mother. But the clincher, for me anyway, was the body of the world's unlikeliest hero. It had fur all over its torso. And search as I might, even under the "hair," I could find no imprint which warranted protection from the wrath of Universal. The charge of imitation, admittedly, was weakened considerably though by the absence of any actual resemblance to the real E.T. Yet, the point remains that this and similar atrocities are apparently selling and possibly even quite well.

In late October 1982, the *New York Times* ran full-page ads informing imitators that they would have to "tell it to the judge." Manufacturers of E.T. items were told very sternly that anyone using the image or name of E.T. without permission would be subject to prosecution. The threatening message informed any involved in such practices that it simply wasn't worth taking the chance.

A UPI article out of New York mentioned on October 23, 1982, that an E.T. crime wave was sweeping the country. It referred to four warehouses in New York alone that had been filled with "bootlegged E.T. dolls, statues, and other paraphernalia the company seized." An attorney for MCA-Universal was quoted as saying that 300 investigations were underway into the manufacture and sale of unlicensed products and that several arrest warrants were to be issued.

This rather sobering news caused me to wonder where I really stood in respect to the studio's legal plans for me. What I especially noted in the UPI story was the number of people or companies that were seen as suspicious, namely 300. I couldn't help thinking about that as a reminder of the Spartan defenders of the pass of Thermopylae in 480 B.C. Granted, there is a world of difference between the vast Persian hordes and the belligerent studio. And, of course, there is the notable divergence between the ignoble and the noble. What most sunk in was the memory that Leonidas' warriors being annihilated, all 300 of them. How I wish that figure cited in the story about the *E.T.* offenders had been something other than the exact number of very dead Spartans!

I tried to imagine that possibly one of them might have managed to escape his fate in that ancient battle. I could have been encouraged then to believe that I may also have had a chance to miss the scrutiny of those litigious eyes in Hollywood (specifically Universal City, California). But the remarkable truth of the matter is that I, in most un-Spartan-like fashion, did manage to avoid prosecution. The surprise for me appeared near the end of the same newspaper story about the "pirates." It said, "Millar's problem never ended in court when an attorney for MCA told the professor recently that the studio was not going to press the case." Could one of the 300 actually have been saved? Wonder of wonders! But hold for a minute here...nobody, and certainly not an attorney, told me anything. And if he spoke to someone, then to whom? And when did he do so? Something told me I better pay another visit to my lawyer.

As I was driving back to my lawyer's office, I heard Neil

Diamond's "Heartlight" on the radio. So much of the song seemed to be based on the plot of *E.T.* While listening, I felt irony in the difficulties that even a star could have by using Universal's story of the special visitor who needed a home. I recalled reading that Neil Diamond wanted to make a specific reference to E.T. but had been prohibited by the studio from doing so. Without being able to explain why, I felt calmer than I had for quite a while. After all, the song still seemed successful without violating any rules. And yet its message of a boy's dream, a need of friendship and a special place, or even an image of "flight" across the moon remained intact. The movie's inspiration obviously affected a tremendous cross-section of the population.

As I arrived at Jack Gibson's office, I entered his waiting room with the throaty strains of "Heartlight" still residing in my head. It's as if the theme of the song encouraged me even more to pursue the specifically Christian interpretation that had sparked my initial controversy with the moviemakers. Maybe I should have let my readers guess, as Neil Diamond had done, who was similar to Jesus in all these ways. I had been too obvious, especially with that sketch on the cover. All I needed to say was that a popular movie (unnamed, of course) reminds me of someone who should be better known than he is. Funny, isn't it, how the mind seems to work quickly under different levels of stress? But all this "weaselly" thinking, I was soon to learn, was quite unnecessary. All I needed was a little time to get an update from my lawyer because he had talked with Universal's attorney, John Nuanes.

As I entered Jack's office to speak about what he might know, I reflected on the many unusual events that brought me to this point. Nothing in the way of my life experience could have forecast anything like what was actually happening. Here I sat in a state of nervous agitation across the desk from a former high school cross-country teammate having no idea what the newspaper article meant when it indicated that one person, only one from among 300, was not to be "pursued" by the legal division of Universal-MCA. And yet, my "offense" was probably better known than anyone's by that date. I decided to let my lawyer friend have the first word.

Actually, it was more an expression than anything verbal. Something on the order of a smirk ... mischievous but not foreboding. I felt more palpitations, shimmering rays of hope I had sensed while hearing Neil Diamond a few minutes earlier. Yet there was no reason for me to feel that I was in any way off the hook. Not quite.

And so Jack spoke, "Al, I've talked to their attorney, Mr. Nuanes. In fact, we had a good conversation, even a few laughs." Oh, what a fraternity these legal types have developed for themselves, I was thinking, with as much malevolence as possible. Profiting from the troubles of those not so fortunate as to know their jargon and their methods. Having a little fun with me and my potentially wrecked career. Being as discreet as possible, I silently permitted Jack his fun with me. He went on.

"Mr. Nuanes has said that nothing in his memory has stirred up people against his studio as much as the publicity that your booklet received. They felt like real heavies in this and, although appreciative of your intentions, did not like being cast in such an unfavorable light by the media. Calls and letters have been received on your behalf. People wanted them to call off the dogs. Some even spoke of boycotting the movie and its products."

Jack Gibson's words were sinking in with intense immediacy. They were getting very mixed reviews, however, as I pondered their significance. Yes, I thought, the people, the support of Christian America, I desperately needed. And I appreciated deeply each effort expended on my behalf. But what really was the studio planning for me now? I listened further.

"The studio has been inundated with requests to license any

manner of items to sell related to *E.T.* It has had to be very careful in dealing with anyone or anything who is selling something that does not have the specific permission of Universal. Your telegram of September 21 was one of many that got sent at the time. You simply were part of a 'shotgun' effect and got hit as hard as someone selling a bogus doll for $25 or more."

I tried to mumble an interruption here about the "break-even" nature of my "business" with E.T. since I was paying for stamps, the printing, and the envelopes to send out copies to the people who requested them. I wondered if the absence of profit would make any difference. Anyway, Jack had saved the best for last.

"According to Mr. Nuanes, Universal Studios sees what you have done, based on current information they have received, as an academic interpretation of the movie and that they have no interest in causing legal difficulties."

Something about the expression "academic interpretation" really pleased me. It sounded very similar to "academic freedom." All the concern I formerly felt about my plight instantly ebbed. And, of course, all the preparations of my many supporters who had been planning a major First Amendment confrontation with the studio were dashed. Universal did the one thing which would settle the issue as painlessly as anyone could have imagined. They were understanding at last. In fact, they even sounded nice. Perhaps this is what we'd expect from the makers of *E.T.* No longer was it a case of, "Professor, call the studio."

I had written to them; they had "written" to me. Maybe the score was pretty even after all. And so I had kindled a little more interest in the already successful movie, gotten some wide coverage through the media, received letters from several people all over (including Ed McMahon), and made many new friends whom I would not have had contact with in more normal circumstances. All this came from "*E.T.*"— *You're More Than a Movie Star,* not even five printed pages! The bomb remained undetonated; the flea endured yet.

## CHAPTER FIVE
## The First Edition

Now that I'm "legal," I should present the pamphlet that created the stir when news of Universal's displeasure was made known. Almost all readers of it seem to feel that an amazing case of overkill was enacted upon what I had written. As I mentioned, I was attempting to move quickly while the masses of people were attending *E.T.* for the first time in mid-summer, 1982. I was unable to flesh out the list of 33 parallels; nor was I able to offer more explanations of what the New Testament reminders were when I realized the closeness of the movie script to the Bible. By presenting the material just as I had originally developed it, I am sharing exactly what many others have seen and commented on since July 1982. Judgement of its validity obviously rests with each reader.

I hope by now that I have recounted the amazing developments that this small piece of writing brought to my own life. I offer in advance apologies to anyone who might take offense or raise a charge of heresy against my treatment of the movie character as having certain attributes reminiscent of Jesus Christ. I wrote all this as I felt it; and as I explained earlier, I responded to an almost compulsive urge to share what I had written with others. Several thousand copies of the pamphlet later, I now offer the original *"E.T."—You're More Than a Movie Star* for the patient readers of the "book version:"

## "E.T."—You're More Than a Movie Star
### *Dr. Al Millar*

The Riddle of E.T.

E.T. —who are you?

Or, rather, who are you like?

For you seem to have had some sort of extra-terrestrial existence, a really long time somewhere else.

And your earliest times on Earth were spent in hiding, almost "submerged" you seemed to be;

Because you showed what you could do when you wanted, like spinning spheres in the air, or when you could, you communicated with "home," wherever that is.

And I watched you heal both plant and man or even "fly."

How'd you learn to resist Newton's law?

And even take others with you when you wished.

Is it an aura; is it—magic?

You've got the power, E.T.

As I recall, you also got involved with an alcoholic beverage (but it wasn't wine).

And, yes, I even saw you wear a robe.

Your followers had to "deny" you to others for a time, but they later got much more dedicated as they all began to accept their special visitor from beyond.

And, yes, those new friends were a big help when the earthly powers that be came looking and even started cutting on you. And you lost blood—DNA and all.

Sad it was to see you lying wounded and rejected near those rocks and even sadder to see you in your suffering calling out to a "Mom" named Mary.

(Even if she was Elliott's, not your own.)

And, E.T., that ESP or mind control — could you be omniscient? Close anyway, I would say. It's more than just plain smart.

And I really must ask you, E.T.—

Did you "die" that Elliott might live?

And after you did, how'd you get the "light" to shine once more?

How did you live again after they put you in your "tomb?" Even there I think I saw that shining light.

And before you ascended from this earth, I heard you say, "I'll be right here. And Elliott knew the truth. Even when you said, "Stay!" he knew you'd say, "Come!"

E.T, if I might summarize, you came to little children, you healed, you created, you wept, you suffered from authorities, you bled, you died, you lived again, you rose, and you left a little reminder in the sky—a rainbow.

E.T., you sound mighty special to those who think.

You sound like love.

You act like yet another special guest.

He would understand.

I hope we do.

The Solution?

Gently tugging at those plant samples, being with bunnies and deer, even briefly with a beneficent raccoon, E.T. is peacefully one with nature, our nature, our world. But his origins are elsewhere both in regard to space and time, almost infinitely distant from earth in both dimensions.

E.T. is introduced to the movie audience diligently "working" the woodlands to help stock the laboratory of his "Christmas decoration" spacecraft. Only with the arrival of groups of men carrying lights in the night does he show fear and apprehension over his being stranded in his new and apparently hostile environment. His earliest solitary experience on earth depicts him as forsaken and dejected. This he remains until his "discovery" by Elliot in the reeds or high grass near where he will be briefly housed by his young protector.

Throngs of movie-goers in the summer of 1982 have marveled at the ingenuity of Steven Spielberg's classic *E.T. the Extra—Terrestrial*. And as record-setting crowds attended each showing, more people than ever in the history of the medium shared poignant moments of fear, pathos, humor, and even affection with the "creature" known as E.T. But what has most amazed me, as a professor of Biblical literature, is the almost uncanny number of parallels that E.T. shares with Jesus. To clarify my position, I have developed the following list of the most obvious characteristics that this most successful piece of entertainment shares with the most remarkable personality who has ever lived. Whether these are developed unconsciously or by design is open to debate, but the sheer numbers of similarities between E.T. and Jesus are really worth considering. Who knows? Perhaps we have at least one way of understanding the popularity of E.T. He really does seem to be more than just another Hollywood creation, a great deal more.

Examine the following attributes of E.T. as they relate to the Scriptural accounts of Jesus:

1. E.T. had a prior extra-terrestrial existence.
2. His early life on earth was "submerged" or hidden.
3. He came to little children.
4. The three admirers (Elliott, Gertie, and Michael) knelt before him. This occurred when E.T. had run to the closet after being frightened by the little girl. (And can that really be a stained-glass window we see behind than?)
5. E.T. had occasion to feel rejected and forsaken on earth.
6. E.T. had a reverence for nature and was seen with "passive" animals such as rabbits and deer.
7. Groups of men pursued him carrying lights and weapons in the night. One thinks of Gethsemane here.
8. E.T. also had an "involvement" with an alcoholic beverage. People still celebrate Christ's turning the water to wine.
9. Yet he was innocent of any wrongdoing.
10. He spun spheres in space in imitation of our solar system.
11. He healed the physical pains of those who loved him. No one can forget E.T.'s response to, "Ouch!"
12. He caused a plant to wither. Matthew 21:19 says that Jesus caused a fig tree to be "withered away. "
13. E.T. wore a robe.
14. And as he emerged from the van after regaining life, he is shrouded in white. The transfiguration of Jesus is described in terms of His "white raiment" (Matthew 17:2).
15. E.T. communicated with "home."
16. He also was seen lying wounded and rejected.
17. E.T.'s followers for a time denied his existence to others. This is especially visible in the bus stop scene.

18. Later, E.T. enjoyed absolute dedication from his followers. Many who had mocked the "goblin" helped him reach "home."
19. E.T. encountered much trouble from governmental authorities. In this case, U.S. Government rather than Roman or Hebrew.
20. E.T. emitted a light, even from his "tomb."
21. E.T. wept. Another "Ouch!"
22. He seemed the epitome of love, even returning the gifts of Elliott.
23. E.T. had the capacity of defying gravity and could "hold" others up with him. Peter's faith kept him above the waves with Jesus when He walked on the water.
24. E.T. possessed a kind of ESP. He had a method of nonverbal communication that seemed to be a form of omniscience. He even knew he was going home at the time of his earthly death.
25. While E.T. was suffering and dying, he called out, "Mom." Of course, she was Elliott s mother, but her name, interestingly enough, is Mary.
26. E.T. died. And note that the doctor pronounced him dead at 15:36 (3:36 p.m.). It is especially significant to recall that the Gospels place the death of Jesus on the cross at some brief time after the "ninth hour" (Matthew 27:45). The Hebrew day began at 6 a.m. so the ninth hour would have been 3 p.m.
27. And it seems that E.T. had to die so that Elliott could live.
28. But E.T. attained resurrection from death, Elliott declared, "He's alive!"
29. And afterwards to Gertie, E.T. said, "Be good."
30. To Elliott, his most beloved follower, he said while touching the boy's temple, "I'll be right here."

31. He also said in his final moments on Earth to Elliott, "Come." Matthew 14:29 reads, "And he said, Come."
32. E.T. ascended to his original "home."
33. And when E.T. returns to his origins we all can see a rainbow flashing across the sky.

Dare we ask, Mr. Spielberg, if there is to be a "Second Coming?"

And this, believe me, is it, the entire text that changed my life for quite some time. For many, reading the little study it is a case of, "I can't believe I read the whole thing." But, after all, brevity is considered a virtue according to Poe and many others. The point here is that what's done is done, and I have been dealing with the effects for which *"E.T."—You're More Than a Movie Star* is unquestionably the cause.

The reactions to my writing the analogy have been almost totally positive, and what has pleased me to no end is the number of ministers and priests who had sent their reactions to me. One Lutheran minister and religious TV talk-show host even ordered 300 copies to be distributed to young people at a church conference. Several nuns have requested copies as well to aid them in teaching confirmation classes or Sunday school classes. I've even heard of several Baptist churches who have used the pamphlet as a teaching tool for Sunday school classes of young people to interest them in the correlation that does exist between modern entertainment and the truths of the New Testament. It's become a kind of religious quest where adolescents in particular go to *E.T.* to see how many parallels to Jesus they can find. Adding to my own delight is the occasional letter from a student somewhere suggesting that the very number of E.T./Jesus parallels, 33, is Biblically significant since that is the accepted age of Jesus at the time of His "going home."

Even several major religious leaders have written letters to me which kindly thank me for the insights I have brought to fans of the movie. I was especially touched by very responsive replies from the Catholic Bishop of Sacramento and Pat Robertson of the 700-Club. I not only feel ecumenical when hearing from the diverse religious groups, I also feel somehow more "legitimized" than I ever did by Universal. I might even feel sanctioned now that I have positive written evidence from so many within the family of Christians.

One thing I've been wanting to do for a while now is present more complete Biblical explanations for each of the original attributes I noticed while attending the movie. Possibly the affinities that exist between E.T. and Jesus will be seen even more clearly if I redo the original list as follows:

1. Estimates of E.T.'s existence before visiting Earth range in the millions of light years, but the divine quality of Jesus includes infinity. His being of heavenly origins and His existing prior to Creation are staggering dimensions for human understanding. So the similarity of a long, long prior extraterrestrial existence seems to be an obvious parallel.

2. E.T. was only accidentally "discovered" on Earth after his spacecraft made a hasty departure. And Jesus, after the miraculous events of His birth, seems to have remained in the humble circumstances of Joseph and Mary and surfaces in the Scriptures only once prior to His beginning His ministry at approximately 30 years of age. Luke 2: 42-50 describes the familiar visit to His "Father's house" in Jerusalem when He was twelve.

3. E.T.'s strongest support obviously came from children, Elliott leading the list. Jesus' involvement with chil-

dren is seen in Matthew 19:14, "Suffer little children, and forbid them not, to come unto me." One could say that E.T. initiated his contact with children because of his acceptance of the candy proffered by Elliott.

4. The image of the three children gazing in wonder at E.T. when he was in the closet reminded me of the visit of the wise men (magi) to the infant Jesus. Of course, the Scriptures do not specify that there were three or that they were kings as legend describes them. Matthew 2:11 describes them as they "fell down" before the child as they presented their gifts.

5. E.T. did seem hurt and abandoned after the night he had communicated with "home." In several instances, Jesus relates such feelings of loss as He did in Matthew 25:42: "For I was hungry, and ye gave me no food; I was thirsty, and ye gave me no drink." And in His most isolated moments on the cross, Jesus uttered, "My God, my God, why hast thou forsaken me?" (Matthew 27:46)

6. One thinks of Jesus' origins on earth as being associated with peaceful animals such as sheep and cattle. Also, we sense constantly His mastery over the forces of nature. E.T. was even able to make his peace with the family dog once he was housed by Elliott.

7. In the Scriptural accounts of the evening in Gethsemane such as in Mark 14, those who pursued Jesus carried "swords and staves" to be certain to capture their prey. E.T. is able to elude the men who scour the woods looking for him.

8. Many people feel that I was really "reaching" when I drew a parallel between E.T.'s beer drinking and Christ's conversion of the water to wine during the marriage

feast in Cana (John 2). I mentioned the "involvement" with alcoholic beverages, but obviously there are startling differences in the circumstances associated with Coors beer and wedding wine. An orthodox Jewish wedding just couldn't be complete without the wine. But a real clue to this parallel occurs in the movie when Gertie tunes in to *Sesame Street*. As we hear a range of B words, including "boy" (E.T.'s first spoken English), the voice on the program also says, "bottles of wine." I really wondered about what the message to the kiddies was. A Bible student of mine was really eager to point this out to me because he hadn't liked this analogy originally.

9. E.T., being unaware of worldly snares, remains innocent. And Jesus, being sinless, is beautifully described in 1 John 3:3 as follows: "And every man that hath this hope in him purifieth himself even as he is pure."

10. As creator of all things, Jesus is seen as prophesying the Kingdom Age in Isaiah 17: "For, behold, I create new heavens and a new earth. E.T.'s amazing feat with the pieces of fruit when he sent them spinning in the air looked like a mini-planetarium. This is, of course, only the tiniest form of "creation" on the part of Elliott's visitor.

11. My initial suggestion that E.T. had similarities to Jesus came when Elliott cut his finger on the buzz saw blade and was touched by the healing finger. Among the many accounts of healing described in the New Testament, the one in Matthew 8:7 seems especially appropriate here: "And Jesus saith unto him, I will come and heal him."

12. E.T. did seem to have a kind of control over plants. One in particular would flourish or wither in conjunction with his own health. Jesus, as a lesson in faith for the disciples, commented on a fig tree that produced only leaves. Matthew 21:19 reads: "Let no fruit grow on thee hence forward forever. And presently the fig tree withered away."

13. Of course, among the costume changes assigned to E.T. is Elliott's robe. This is prominent in the kitchen scene. Naturally, Jesus would have worn the standard clothing of his era, a long robe. Several references to His "garment" or its hem can be found. Matthew 9:20 describes the diseased woman who knew she would be whole again if she "touched the hem of his garment. "

14. The chronology doesn't work completely in the analogy of the white shroud that E.T. wears after regaining life when compared with the Transfiguration of Jesus. As described in Matthew 17:2, "Jesus' raiment was as white as the light." Granted, this is not a parallel of two resurrections; it is one of white apparel. I had to employ the only Scriptural reference I could find to the color of the "aura" associated with the appearance of Jesus as a glorified being.

15. E.T.'s communication device, energized by the winds of nature, allows him to contact "home" so he will be reunited with his own kind. I saw a significant parallel here to the several prayers Jesus uttered as He wished to produce a verbal link with His Father above. The most poignant prayer is also done in a natural setting, the Garden of Gethsemane, and reveals Jesus' agonizing sense of isolation. Matthew 26:39 presents the prayer that no Christian ever forgets: "O my Father, if it be

possible, let this cup pass from me." I found the desire to project beyond the immediate realm of existence to be a powerful need in both the movie and the Bible.

16. When Michael locates E.T. lying so ill near the stream, I got the impression that he is willfully preparing himself to break the bond that holds him to Elliott and the earth. E.T. lies pale and bruised prior to his death. I considered the descriptions of the Crucifixion including the scourging and battering that preceded the nailing of Jesus to the cross. Any reader of the dread events associated with the death of Jesus is aware of His willfully permitting the treatment that has him call out that he is forsaken by his own Father (Mark 15:34).

17. Elliott's motivation in denying his relationship with the "goblin" at the bus stop was of course related to protecting his new friend. During the trial of Jesus prior to His execution, Peter denies his own relationship with the Lord three different times. He said in Mark 14:71 as he cursed and swore: "I know not this man of whom ye speak." His reason for his actions was obviously a selfish sense of preserving himself from persecution.

18. The entire group of adolescents associated with Elliott and Michael ultimately rallied around E.T. to help him reach the sanctuary of his spacecraft. After the tumultuous events of Jesus' Crucifixion and Resurrection, His followers supported His cause through torture and martyrdom. Peter, immediately after denying Jesus, wept when he "called to mind the word that Jesus said unto him, 'Before the cock crows twice, thou shalt deny me thrice'" (Mark 14:72).

19. The sealing of Elliott's home by representatives of the

U. S. Government and the attempts by authorities to preclude E.T.'s returning "home" seemed analogous to the difficulties Jesus encountered not only from the local manifestations of the Roman Empire in Israel but also from representatives of the Jews' own controlling sects and parties. The essential groups He dealt with in Israel were the Herodians, the Sadducees, and the Pharisees (Matthew 22: 15-46). Finally, Jesus is delivered over to Pilate by the Sanhedrin. The reference I made to Hebrew authorities in this parallel represented the wide range of troubles Jesus had from His own people.

20. E.T.'s heartlight has become one of his most renowned features, visible on just about every doll or likeness available. I was particularly interested in seeing the red glow from this most special feature when he was placed in the container by the scientists after his death. So also is intense light associated with the Resurrection of Jesus. When the angel rolled back the stone from His tomb, "His countenance was like lightning, and his raiment white as snow" (Matthew 28:3). Luke goes on to describe two men in "shining garments" who spoke of the risen Jesus (24:4).

21. E.T. revealed that his emotions were quite affected by his upcoming separation from Elliott, and he is shown shedding tears as he moves to his spaceship. When Lazarus became fatally ill, prior to his being raised from death by Jesus, John provided the shortest verse in the Bible by giving His reaction to news of His friend's death: "Jesus wept" (John 11:35).

22. One of the reasons for the incredible popularity *E.T.* has obtained is the reciprocal nature of love. E.T. embodies warmth and generosity; thus, others wish to share in

these feelings. One of the Bible's most eloquent statements on the subject of love is the words of Jesus: "A new commandment I give unto you, that ye love one another; as I have loved you, that ye also love one another" (John 13:34).

23. Certainly, among the most interesting aspects of the movie is E.T.'s uncanny ability to float above the earth or to cause objects and even people to do the same. It is probable that the scene in Matthew 15 where Jesus walks upon the waves and then encourages Peter to join Him is a certain indication that no natural law can be applicable.

24. E.T. most certainly maintained a kind of psychic link with Elliott and possessed a level of intelligence that seemed other worldly. Omniscience as an attribute of His divinity is revealed in several ways as the Scriptures record even the child Jesus as "filled with wisdom" (Luke 2:40). Even at twelve, Jesus "amazed" His teachers with "his understanding and answers" (Luke 2:47).

25. While E.T. remained on Earth, the only mother he had any contact with, Elliott's, just happened to be named Mary. John's Gospel relates that in His most intense suffering prior to dying on the cross Jesus saw His mother standing nearby. He spoke to her in the common form of addressing females: "Woman, behold thy son" (John 20:26). While E.T. does call out to Mary, I find it at least interesting that he uses a familiar term, "Mom," in addressing her. As ill as E.T. is, this is one of the more touching scenes in the movie.

26. The Synoptic Gospels (Matthew, Mark, and Luke) employ the Hebrew reckoning for time, 6 a.m. indi-

cating the first hour and so forth. But the Gospel of John uses Roman time with the new "day" beginning at midnight as we do now. Either way of figuring time, all the Gospels clearly place the time of the Crucifixion at six hours in duration beginning at the Hebrew third hour, or 9 a.m. Death occurred after 3 p.m. in every account, so the statement in the movie that E.T. is pronounced dead at 15:36 (3:36 p.m.) really seems to be a clear indication of the probable parallels that do exist on this point.

27. Both E.T. and Elliott are simultaneously ailing near the end of the movie, and even the latter seems near death until E.T. severed the unity that had been established between them. He had to die so that the boy would recover. In only a miniscule way, E.T. typifies the ultimate Sacrificial act described in I Corinthians 5:7 by Paul: "For even Christ, our Passover, is sacrificed for us."

28. As excited as Elliott was over the discovery that E.T. returned to life, this aspect of the movie is but a pale reminder of the magnificence the Gospel writers assign to the Resurrection of Jesus. Not only did "a vision of angels, who said that he was alive" (Luke 24:23), announce the risen Jesus, but the Scriptures record many physical details of Him alive. Jesus even had to discount the opinion that He was only a spirit when He appeared to the eleven remaining disciples: "Behold ... that it is I myself ... flesh and bones" (Luke 24:39).

29. E.T.'s simple admonition to Gertie about being good is amplified in a significant verse in 3 John 11: "Follow not that which is evil, but that which is good. He that doeth good is of God, but he that doeth evil hath not seen God.

30. The precise Biblical parallel to E.T.'s parting words as he suggested a continuing presence between himself and Elliott is among the most obvious. The last verse of the book of Matthew gives Jesus' words as follows: "Lo, I am with you always, even unto the end of the world. Amen" (28:20).

31. The link that exists between E.T. and Elliott brings the invitation for the boy to join his alien comrade in "Home." A somewhat similar invitation is extended to Peter. when he states "Lord, if it be thou, bid me come unto thee on the water (Matthew 14:28). Jesus replied simply, "Come." It was only the fear Peter had for his own safety (as well as an instant diminishment of his faith) that caused him to sink below the waves. I find it interesting that neither Elliott nor Peter originally had the slightest doubt that he would be able to join his respective friend in a most unfamiliar element — space or water.

32. The rising heavenward of E.T.'s spacecraft is the last event of his visit to earth. His ascension is a type reminiscent of the final event of Jesus' mission on earth. Luke describes the Messianic Ascension as follows: "And it came to pass, while he blessed them, he was parted from them, and carried up into heaven" (24:51).

33. I was much impressed by the rainbow that flashes behind E.T.'s vanishing spacecraft in the last frames of the movie. It obviously adds a great deal to the nighttime sky as the audience remains awash in emotion. God's covenant with Noah (and with mankind) that He would not flood the earth again is the earliest Scriptural reference to a rainbow (Genesis 9:12). But an even more beautiful description of this natural phenom-

enon is found in the Old Testament book of Ezekial: "Like the appearance of the bow that is in the cloud in the day of rain, so was the appearance of the likeness of the glory of the Lord" (1: 28).

Perhaps my study of *E.T.* as a Christian parable doesn't really demonstrate that its star is a "likeness ... of the Lord," but I do feel as I have from its first showing that the movie has a highly suggestive quality. Whether the screenwriter, Melissa Mathison, or the director, Steven Spielberg, intended to employ the "Greatest Story Ever Told" will probably never be known. But ruling out the possibility of immensely successful coincidences, I feel that someone really knew what he or she was doing when the E.T./Jesus identities were developed. I quickly detected 33 parallels between Jesus and E.T. and have now attempted to amplify each here should anyone wish to follow how I originally perceived them. But now that half a year has passed since I wrote the pamphlet, I am convinced that there's even more to this "movie star" than what I first met E.T. Certainly, more than 33 similarities to Jesus do exist.

## CHAPTER SIX
## The Second Edition

My contention that the movie *E.T.* contains even more parallels to Christianity is something I sense more strongly as time continues to pass. When I wrote my original list, I considered only, to me, the most obvious indications that the script leaned strongly on the New Testament. What amazed me later in reflecting on all of this is that there are possibly even earlier analogies to E.T. in the Old Testament because there are prophetic statements which many believers accept as anticipating the arrival of Jesus centuries later. To illustrate, I quote from Isaiah 53:2 where certain physical features of the Messiah are presented: "... he hath no form nor comeliness, and when we shall see him, there is no beauty that we should desire him."

The initial sight of E.T. brings to most people just about the same shock that it did to Elliott during their first encounter near his home. But the real message of both the Scripture here and the movie is that the physical appearance is ultimately irrelevant. That there is "no beauty" is, of course, only the shallowest response that we can make to anyone. Nothing ever affected Elliott more positively in his brief life that could come close to his friendship with an alien whose initial outward appearance could almost lacerate the eyeball. Knowing him changes this attitude very quickly, however.

Another Old Testament verse very specifically isolated the differentiation between the external and inner qualities that all of us possess. It's so germane that I'm almost tempted to suggest that the antecedent of "his" could apply to E.T. himself. "Look not on his countenance, or on the height of his stature ... For man looketh on the outward appearance, but the Lord looketh on the heart." (Samuel 16: 7)

All *E.T.* moviegoers really participate in this remarkable insight regarding E.T. because his heart is among his most visible aspects. E.T. evokes an important kind of sympathy, as many special people do, because of his remarkable differences from normal people, any people.

As amazing as it seems, a passage in Isaiah describing the abuse which would come to the Suffering Servant (Jesus in most people's opinion) actually offers a fascinating analogy to the physical appearance of E.T. It reads: "As many were astounded at thee — his visage was so marred more than any man, and his form more than the sons of man — " (52:14). The uncanny similarity of this description to the alien's own features draws even closer in the note to this verse found in the Scofield Reference Bible. "The literal rendering presents a shocking picture: 'so marred from the form of man was his aspect that his appearance was not that of a son of man, 'i.e., not human.'"

While scholars discuss their interpretations of these Old Testament verses as anticipating future troubles for Jesus or Israel herself, I find that the implication of someone who does not have human form has to be one of the most thought-provoking points that could be made about the Biblical analogies to E.T. I became more convinced than ever that the source for the movie had to be a rather liberal injection from many parts of the Bible. After all, one can't even imagine Mr. Spielberg's not having used it before in his pertinent treatment of the Ark of the Covenant in *Raiders of the Lost Ark.* One continues to wonder why other fascinating attributes from the Scriptures couldn't have been employed to produce his most successful movie ever.

For these and many other reasons, I feel that many other concepts and direct borrowings emanate in the "noblest monument of English prose;" the world's record-holding bestseller, the Bible. And so I would like to offer what other similarities I have encountered in *E.T.* to Scriptural descriptions of Jesus and His early Church. Several of them have come from further reflection on the movie itself; others have been suggested by interested viewers of the movie, and a few developed out of my third visit to see *E.T.,* which occurred on February 1, 1983. I was especially interested to see what "new" parallels I might detect after being away from the movie itself for about six months. As my updated list indicates, I feel a slight sense of shame that I wasn't more perceptive before. Here are some of the obvious Biblical parallels I should have seen but didn't:

1. The opening scene of *E.T.* provides a panorama of starry skies which gives a range from the heavens to the woodland setting where the spaceship rests. One can think of the significance of a clear night when Jesus was born in Bethlehem with "a multitude of the heavenly host" (Luke 2:13) announcing the news to the shepherds. It is fitting also that our first view of E.T. on earth is under just such a sky.

2. Also, in the first contact with Elliott, E.T. in returning the ball thrown to him is seen in a stable-like structure separated some distance from a place of residence. Interestingly, a large light (the moon) illuminates the scene from above.

3. One of the most notable supporters of E.T.'s visit to earth is the scientist who was actually attempting to find him in the woods before Elliott had made direct contact. Later, the same man says to Elliott, "He came to me too. I've been wishing for this since I was ten. His being here is a miracle." He also accompanies the family and the now friendly bikers to observe E.T.'s reunion with "Home." This scientist's eager anticipation of E.T.'s visit reminds me of Simeon who in Luke 2:25-35 is depicted as waiting a lifetime to see Jesus. When Simeon finally sees the infant Jesus, he says: "... mine eyes have seen thy salvation, Which thou hast prepared before the face of all people" (30-31). With the best possible spirit, the scientist also told Elliot that he was glad E.T. had come to him even though he had sought such a meeting for so many years.

4. Other very familiar images from the movie became apparent during my last viewing of *E.T.* One of them was especially noticeable in a visual and auditory sense — the prevalence of jingling keys. These were attached to the "chaser" who was trying to flush E.T. out of the brush when he is attempting to get back to his spaceship. I wondered about the symbolism of authority or control keys might indicate. Couldn't they also reflect a kind of mini-weaponry, little swords or daggers? Whatever, they are harsh and metallic and reminded me of the swords carried by pursuers of Jesus in the Gethsemane betrayal by Judas. And later in the movie, one of the men (the same one?) in a spacesuit prior to entering Elliott's home most meticulously stuffs his collection of keys inside his suit. Is it any wonder that Revelation 1:18 refers to "the keys of hell and of death?"

5. Yet another similarity to the Garden of Gethsemane occurs during the Halloween night attempt to "phone home." Elliott, after offering all the assistance he can to help E.T. set up his communicator, is discovered asleep the next morning. And during the night, apparently while his "protector" slept, E.T. was mysteriously harmed and rendered practically helpless. Elliott had in fact lost him in the forest. Jesus had requested that Peter and other disciples "watch with me" (Matthew 26: 38) while He prayed alone to His Father. And yet each time Jesus checked on His disciples during the night, they were "asleep again; for their eyes were heavy" (Matthew 26:43).

6. One of the most remarkable concepts developed by the movie is the choice of the name Elliott. Not only does the name represent the Hebrew word for God in its first two letters EL, but the name itself is derived from the Hebrew name Elijah or in Greek Elias. Even more significant is the fact that when Jesus was dying on the cross, he called out in Aramaic, "Eloi, Eloi, lama sabachthani?" (Mark 15: 34) The word "Eloi" is normally translated "God," but its pronunciation in Aramaic would sound much closer to the name Elijah or Elias. Thus, Elliott's name is directly related to the sound uttered by Jesus in His direst suffering prior to His death. Another name than Elliott couldn't be anywhere nearly so significant to the overall meaning of the movie. This is of immensely greater importance than the mere statement that Elliott's name begins with E. and concludes with T. This is just another point of similarity between the boy and his most special visitor.

7. The name Michael may also have significance to the religious aspect of *E.T.* In the Bible, this is the name of the Archangel (Jude 9; Revelation 12:7). In Hebrew, Michael means, "Who is like God?" It is obvious that Michael's name concludes with the same two letters that form the beginning of Elliott. And the el form is the root of the Hebrew plural Elohim, the most common name for God in the Old Testament. But it is as an angel that the boy Michael seems to have his most vital function in the movie. When Elliott arrives home ill after "losing" E.T. on Halloween night, Michael speeds off to offer aid to the now helpless creature. I find it of special interest that this assistance to E.T. occurs on All Saints' Day, November 1. And a bit later, Michael provides whatever means he can to help E.T. get to the arriving spaceship. His driving the van to the park provides one of the major portions of excitement for the viewers of the movie.

8. Before leaving the area of name symbolism, I should include Gertie to round out the family. As a nickname for Gertrude, the child's name is a bit unusual for the modern era. Actually, the probable most famous use of the full name Gertrude is found in *Hamlet*. The name Shakespeare chose for Hamlet's mother is Gertrude. The name means "all true." Somehow the smallest supporter E.T. has, Gertie, is as true to him as anyone. No one can forget the pleasure she took in dressing him up as her playmate. Also noteworthy is that she told him as she stowed him in her closet for safekeeping to "Be Good." This happens to be exactly what E.T. says to Gertie in his parting statement as he leaves Earth.

9. Also important is Elliott's comment when he discovers

what Gertie has done with E.T. As he sees E.T. in the dress and wig, Elliott exclaims: "Oh God!" I guess most people wouldn't assume too much by this unfortunately overworked expression, but in this movie—who knows?

10. Another scene involving Gertie had more meaning for me in my third trip to the movie. While E.T. heals Elliott's cut finger, Mary is seen reading to her daughter from *Peter Pan* the following words: "Children can get well again if they believe ... " To have the dialogue overheard while a miracle of healing is observed is a really poignant "touch" on the part of Mr. Spielberg. I know—"Ouch!"

11. Those closet scenes offered up yet more to someone tracing Christian parallels in the movie. When Mary looked into Elliott's closet, she saw a variegated assortment of stuffed toys that included, unbeknownst to her, the rigidly set face of E.T. This "fading into the crowd" effect for the purpose of self-preservation reflects a familiar circumstance in the New Testament. On the occasion when the Pharisees were taunting Jesus, John 8:59 says "took they up stones to cast at him; but Jesus hid himself ... going through the midst of them, and so passed by."

12. I was probably even more impressed with the death watch associated with E.T.'s expiration than I had been formerly. Several reasons for this exist, which I'm sure I had recognized subconsciously before. For one, the empathy extended to the suffering friends by Michael and Gertie and, of course, Mary is effectively and skillfully emblematic of the sorrowful observers of Christ's Crucifixion. In addition to a centurion who declared he

was seeing the Son of God, Mark's Gospel mentions "... women looking on afar off, among whom were Mary Magdalene; and Mary, the mother of James the less and of Joses; and Salome" (Mark 15: 39-40).

A second significant detail concerning E.T.'s death was the exercise of will concerning Elliott. He told his earthbound friend to, "Stay." He knew that the youngster's survival depended upon the separation that death would evoke. In this sacrifice, the combined motifs of friendship and love that punctuate the movie so well are beautifully blended. As John says in verse 13 of Chapter 15: "Greater love hath no man than this, that a man lay down his life for his friends." Through E.T.'s suffering, he becomes endeared to all who feel and who love—with the possible exception of *Newsweek's* George Will! He becomes the "man" described by John's Gospel.

The third aspect of the dying episode is even more directly associated with the Biblical description of Christ's ultimate sacrifice on the cross. At the time He expired, the Gospel writers record that "the veil of the temple was torn in two from the top to the bottom" (Mark 15:38). In *E.T.,* we see the doctor very forcefully separating the vinyl curtain that drapes the expired form of our extra-terrestrial. The plastic is opened obviously from the "top to the bottom." It is immediately after this when the doctor "calls it," announcing the time of E.T.'s death at 15:36. I've already mentioned my surprised reaction to this as being almost exactly the same time of the day as Jesus is reported to have died on Good Friday.

Finally, we observe the rapid "entombment" of E.T.

which, just like that of Jesus, is to be temporary. E.T.'s "public" emergence in his "shroud" as he stands in the rear of the van which Michael had driven to the park has an almost mystical quality to it. The boys on the bicycles listen with utter admiration as Elliott announces to them who this visitor from beyond actually is. This scene of the movie has an almost reverential atmosphere of stillness and wonder.

Other parallels to the Biblical accounts of Jesus are also present in *E.T.* They probably do not need a large degree of amplification because it is perhaps the "spirit" of their familiarity that carries them into the Christian consciousness. By listing these as minor details, I don't really intend to minimize their importance; it's just that I want to encourage this kind of analogical thinking among others. I know before starting that my additional items will not exhaust the total possibilities that exist between the movie and the Bible. But I do feel it is worth considering the rest of these "newer" items that did not reach people by means of my pamphlet.

13. E.T. came to the meek. Elliott is seen as something of a wimp by his peers.

14. Before there was any meeting between E.T. and Elliott, the latter "prophesied" exactly what would happen should the "creature" fall into the hands of his pursuers. Elliott said even before E.T. had accepted his gifts of candy that people would want to "experiment" on him. Elliott later accuses the doctors and scientists of "killing E.T."

15. E.T.'s death brought a most meaningful statement from Elliott: "I'll always believe in you. I love you."

16. The Simeon-like scientist said that he had waited for the visit of an E.T. since he was ten. It is interesting at least to notice that Elliott is exactly ten years of age when he meets E.T.

17. At the time of Elliott's discovery of E.T. in the tall grass near his home, there is the effect of an earthquake in the immediate vicinity. Trash cans roll over, and even the swings begin to move in response to the intensity of this original contact between the new arrival and his soon-to-be best friend on Earth. E.T. is definitely no coyote.

18. Almost unnecessary to say is that E.T. changed the lives of those who knew him.

19. As he departs for "Home," I sense an anticipation of a reunion with those who had met E.T. The newspaper accounts tell us that this very well may occur before too many other movies have the Spielberg treatment. The "Second Coming" of E.T. is an eagerly awaited event.

20. I can't resist the suggestion that the most famous initials to come our way since J.R. might have some meaning on their own. The 'E' could very well be short for the common Old Testament word for God, Elohim. And the 'T' actually duplicates the shape of the cross that the Romans used for crucifying victims of their justice. The standard symbol of Christianity is not nearly so accurate as the basic capital T. In this view, E.T. as a name unifies both Testaments. When it comes to independent interpretation, anything's possible.

21. There is also a "supper" attended entirely by male guests in the movie. The reference to "little fishes" during the discussion of pizza made me think, just for a moment, about the feeding of the five thousand with

"but five loaves, and two fishes" (Matthew 14:17). I realize that I'm providing my ultimate "stretch" with this parallel, however.

22. My final analogy comments on the cinematic effectiveness at both the beginning and ending of the movie. As if to show us the heavenly origins of E.T., the sky, as mentioned before, is our first sight once the movie starts. Then the camera focuses on the evergreens of earth. But as the movie concludes, the reverse is true. The camera follows E.T.'s ascension into the evening sky after leaving the woodland setting. Our minds are conscious of the "below to above" direction of E.T.'s and Jesus' journey after visiting Earth. Only a few frames focusing on a very wistful Elliott follow the scene of the spacecraft's rapid exit. And he, too, looks above for what could just be one of the most understated conclusions Hollywood has developed.

Although there is no Biblical support for the idea, I also ought to mention the interest many people have taken in E.T.'s lighted heart region. A number of Roman Catholics and other individuals see this as an emblem of the glowing Sacred Heart. Many have told me that this concept is the among the most meaningful details they carry away from attending the movie. It is significant that E.T.'s heartlight is on when he communicates with "Home," when he regains life in the container provided by the scientists, and when he seems to transfer the glowing energy to his healing finger.

Among the many letters I have received from people offering their own interpretations of parallels are two I cannot avoid mentioning here. One, a former student of mine, Michele Weiner, wrote that she believes E.T. possesses a Jewish nose.

Actually, there is a theory that E.T. might have been created with Menachem Begin as a model.

Another letter I received shortly after news of my near-lawsuit was made public included eighteen different similarities to the Bible. Joe T. of Mesa, Arizona, wanted me to read a list he had developed independent from me. I was pleased to note that we had seen several of the same things in *E.T.,* and I was more aware of the fertile field I sensed for anyone who wished to think in an analogical manner regarding this most amazing movie. With Joe's permission, I'll list eight of his most unusual insights into the story base that he is also certain has its origin in the New Testament. These concepts are worth considering:

1. Joe and his wife wondered about Elliott's freeing the frogs. Neither knew quite how this fit into the concept that night be a Christian parable otherwise. "They represent the release of the sacrificial animals in the temple," she finally concluded. Elliott was acting and thinking as E.T. here.

2. He also saw a kind of sacrament involving the shirt left by Elliott's and Michael's father in the garage where the boys are hunting up parts to make a transmitter. To quote Joe: "If sacrament can be defined as an emblem that is partaken of to remember or honor another, then the shirt incident was an attempt at recreating the same type of emotion."

3. The betrayal kiss.

4. Attempted healing of a sword cut ear.

5. Procession through the streets.

6. The suggestion that the fellow with the keys be named Pete or Simon.

7. Marching Roman soldier impression given by the men rolling the tube up the hill.
8. The sword in the side, represented by the electric shock heart stimulation.

Thanks to Joe, we have even more food for thought regarding what will indubitably become the most popular movie of all time. All I'm really trying to offer is one of the answers to the question, "Why?" And it is a continuing tribute to Mr. Spielberg, Ms. Mathison, and others that the Christian interpretation of *E.T.* is but one of many ways to enjoy the experience of seeing it. I'm told that many psychological and sociological studies will be based on the effect this movie has on so many people. It really is filling a void that has loomed in these times of alienation and violence.

Before closing my chapter on other parallels to the Bible that I and others have recognized, I wish to present my reaction to the last sight we have of E.T. as the entry ramp of the spacecraft retracts over the opening into which he has entered prior to the flight home. E.T. stands silhouetted by the brightly lighted interior of his spacecraft, and the mesh of the ramp folds itself over the opening. As the camera remains focused through the ramp on the receding space of the doorway, I detected in the "grainy" or slightly distorted final view of E.T. yet another possible parallel between him and Jesus. A momentary flash of the Shroud of Turin photographs struck my eyes in the last second I gazed at E.T. Have I gone too far with this one? All anybody has to do is open his or her eyes. Who knows what dividends such an interest in this phenomenal movie experience could bring? I, for one, know that there is a great deal more than a movie star to be found in this loveable little E.T.

As an epilogue to the other specific matters related to my

"controversial" pamphlet, I feel that certain key letters ought to be included here. For many months since the *E.T.*-related events of my life occurred, my mail has proved to be fascinating. Whether I was hearing from a Catholic priest in Japan, a cancer patient in California, a psychology professor in Israel, or from thousands of others who wished to speak of E.T., I have enjoyed my new reading matter. Well, almost all. For in the midst of strong messages of support and shared insights regarding the movie, I did receive one hate letter. I only wish some people could read things through a second time.

But I am still overwhelmed by the positive tone I have found to be in so many other letters and cards that continue even as I write my fuller account of "The Flea." Just today I received this from a thoughtful person:


1/24/1983

Dear Professor Millar,

Thank you for the E.T. booklet you sent me! I found it most enjoyable! Your comparison of E.T. to Jesus was most stimulating. Now I know why I fell in love with the little fellow! He had qualities in him that very few of us have. Maybe our world isn't that bad yet, but its getting there! E.T. inspired us!

E.T. has won the hearts of millions of children all over the world. Also, though they might not want to admit, millions of adults.

Please let me know if you plan to publish any other booklets on E.T. in the future!

Sincerely,
J.G.

From interested individuals, ministers, even additional former students of mine, I'd like to offer what I have selected from their letters as a sample of significant responses people continue to make regarding the movie and my writing on the subject of E.T. and Jesus. Completely at random, they are as follows:

9/27/1982

Dear Professor Millar,

I should like to receive one of your booklets on E.T. I hadn't thought of the Jesus parallel at all but thought it would make an excellent evening's discussion for my women's group after everyone has seen the film.

Good luck in your battle against Universal studios. My husband, who teaches economics at the University of Maryland, said having Universal studios on your back is the best advertisement he can think of for your little pamphlet. He thinks your sales will rival "Gone with the Wind!"

Sincerely,
M.F. (Maryland)

———

11/12/1982

Dear Al,

Thanks for your booklet on E.T. I wish that I had read it before I preached my sermon. You had great insight into the thrust of the movie. I sent a tape to Universal studios and received a curt reply which said, in essence, that they were not interested in hearing the sermon. Keep up the good work.

Sincerely,
P. L. (Kansas)

———

Dear Professor Millar,

I was very interested to read in the *Los Angeles Times* last month of your four-page pamphlet which notes 33 parallels between E.T. and the life of Jesus. I felt quite elated, in fact, because when I saw the film a couple of months ago, I was immediately struck with the parallels — from the discovery of E.T. in that stable like setting to his "ascension" after assuring Elliot, "I will be right here."

I read several reviews of the movie, but found only references to the Good Samaritan story. I was beginning to think that perhaps I had read the Jesus story into the film, but felt there were just too many parallels to ignore.

If your pamphlet constitutes "unfair competition" with the film as Universal asserted, it must be powerful writing indeed!

Sincerely,
A.S. (California)

---

As I continue to ponder all of the events surrounding this single movie and its diverse effects on almost all who see it, I feel fortunate that I have not to date been in more trouble over my actions of July 1982. But I wouldn't have missed the poignant responses from so many for almost anything. As these letters indicate, the movie *E.T.* is a catalyst for exchanging ideas. And more of that sort of thing may be just what the doctor ordered for everyone.

Even now, people suggest that I "do" *Tron* or *The Dark Crystal*. How I hate to admit that I haven't been to see them yet or *Star Wars* either for that matter. And if I do go to other movies that may have a religious base, I'm not sure I'd tell anyone about it next time around. But who knows? The interest is definitely there. And Hollywood may have to strike out for new resources to find their stories. It isn't really their fault they just happen to have started at the top.

Peace to all!

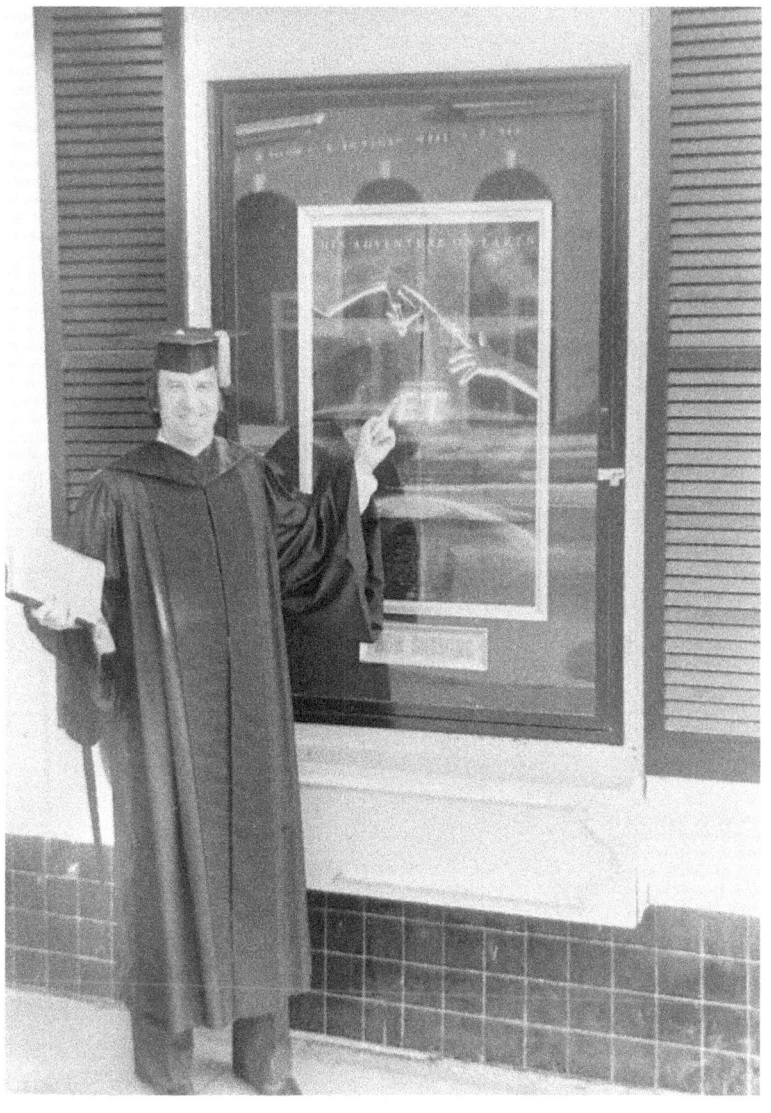

HOLLYWOOD AND THE PROFESSOR: THE FLEA'S REPRIEVE

## AFTERWORD

My Dad died on Friday the 13th, 2000. I was 24 years old. On that fateful Friday morning of the day he passed, he called and asked for his daughters to come and be with him as he thought he would be "leaving" early in the morning. We were by his bedside when Dad closed his eyes and went into a trance-like state. Then, a couple of minutes later, he opened his eyes, looked at all of us and said, "I don't know how to do it." And, of course, we all laughed. His sense of humor was still intact up to the final hour.

I will always be grateful I was there for my Dad until the end. After my father passed, I tried to live what many would consider a normal life in the suburbs. In the end, however, that kind of life didn't suit me. So I moved to the city, went back to school for a master's degree, moved across the country, moved back to the city, and have now finished pursuing a Ph.D. in Public Policy and Administration. My entire career has been in higher education; it has simply felt like home.

My sisters and I continue to share fond memories of Dad. Whether it was his passion for the Dallas Cowboys, watching the sunset, Edgar Allen Poe (or Chaucer!), his sense of humor and quick wit, his ping-pong playing, or his dramatic personality. He may hold the record for the most "Dad sneeze" that ever sneezed.

He was the most joyful, caring, supportive and loving Dad — our hero and best friend. He still put us first, even when he was fighting the good fight. I don't think he had one good day or even maybe a few good hours in the timespan of those last two years. At least we can say we knew him, we loved him, and we can live in our special memories ... and now, through this book which has brought his voice and humor alive again.

Today, I often wonder what kinds of conversations we would have. We would probably disagree on important topics like religion and politics, but one thing is for sure, our conversations would be interesting! Especially from one professor to another.

*— Heather E. Millar, Ph.D. MBA*

Dr. Albert Millar saw Messianic parallels in 'E.T.'
Tract led film studio to consider legal action
T-D Photo

## Studio's threat over use of E.T. propels professor

By Wilford Kale
Times-Dispatch State Staff

NEWPORT NEWS — "E.T. The Extra-Terrestrial" has made Dr. Albert Millar of Christopher Newport College something of a celebrity.

A controversy involving the English professor and Universal City Studios, which owns the rights to the movie produced by Steven Spielberg, has focused a national spotlight on Dr. Millar. The point of the conflict is a five-page tract on "E.T." that Dr. Millar wrote and published.

The pamphlet — "'E.T.' — You're More Than a Movie Star" — presents a list of 33 similarities between E.T.'s life and the life of Jesus Christ. About 400 copies were printed.

In an interview Friday, Dr. Millar, a self-professed fundamentalist, said he had never before been so moved "to share my feelings. I felt this movie had a deeper meaning and that I should write the pamphlet and that people should know what I have uncovered. I just had to tell people."

After completing the pamphlet in July he mailed a copy to

## HOLLYWOOD AND THE PROFESSOR: THE FLEA'S REPRIEVE

# The Captain's Log

VOLUME XIV, NUMBER 6 — CHRISTOPHER NEWPORT COLLEGE — OCTOBER 8, 1982

## Dr. Millar faces possible E.T. lawsuit

*Dr. Al Millar*

by Pat Andrews

The following interview occurred on September 29, 1982. Originally scheduled two weeks earlier, it had to be delayed because of legal considerations. Present during the interview were Dr. Al Millar, Ellen Rockwell, a colleague, and Pat Andrews, representing The Captain's Log.

*What exactly is your infamous pamphlet about, Dr. Millar?*

"Well, it reflects a response that I made to seeing E.T., which I've seen two times total, my first viewing of it was when I first took the children in the summer, and had 24 similarities in mind when I finished looking at the movie. When I saw it a second time, I added, I suppose, the other nine. Some people think there's a significance there."

*These are similarities to Christ?*

"They're similarities to Jesus that I see in the character of E.T. and the grand total of 33 is what I produced in the booklet."

"Well, you know I was on this talk show in San Antonio a few hours ago... Supposedly there's to be a ski concerning this on Saturday Night Live; this is a new one; this is the latest... yeah. It's unbelievable how this thing has gone."

*How has the publicity affected you; do you feel it's had a positive effect, or has it —*

"There's been some tension in the home, because my children are accustomed to talking on the phone for great lengths of time, and now the phone calls are for Daddy, and they cannot imagine why anybody would want to talk to this man... nobody said anything to him before, for years. Why now do people call up Daddy?"

*Do you think it's affected your teaching career at all?*

"Well, I have continued to make teaching foremost among anything I do, so I have to put people aside, do my preparation, do my grading – I run on about three or four tracks most of the time, so, um, you'd have to check with students on whether they've seen any diminishment in my ability to teach. I suppose I'm not a judge of that!"

*Can you give an example of a couple of the Christ/E.T. similarities you've found – other*

than those mentioned in the Daily Press?

"Let's see... I wonder if the Press mentioned that both E.T. and Jesus wear robes. I did notice that. That's very minor. Both, of course, had involvement with an alcoholic beverage: in the case of E.T. it's the humorous scene with the beer, and then people celebrate the first miracle concerning Jesus.

"The most major similarity, I do believe, is that the time of death for E.T. was listed at 15:36 or 3:36 p.m., and in regard to the Scriptural account, it is shortly after, what, the ninth hour, I believe, which is 3 p.m. in the Hebrew day."

*What motivated you to go see E.T.?*

"Children. I'm not a science fiction buff, so – I still have never seen Star Wars."

Rockwell asks, "Are you destroying all your copies?" Millar responds in a loud whisper, "No! No! Not yet, we still they really come down on me. Supposedly, I'm going to be on CBS at ten minutes 'til 7 [p.m.]; they're going to call me... Have you seen the movie yet?"

"No... We tried to, but it was sold out Sunday," says Rockwell.

"Well, it's caused such publicity for the movie that they will probably do considerably more business than they have done," says Millar.

*I know that a lot of students have gone to see the movie again, to find out where you got your ideas.*

"Oh, yes. Yet, I'm still apparently being crucified because of this."

*Which parts of the movie, without giving the plot away, did you find most effective on a personal level?*

"I was immensely impressed with the scene that I usually compare to the Transfiguration. It is when E.T. has been resurrected, has been placed in a van, and then after a chase scene, he emerges, draped in what appears to be a white shroud. And there is mist, and a special lighting effect. That was, I thought, a very effective part of the movie. Many people are in awe of the defying of gravity, and the movement of the bikes across the full moon – um, I guess I was not as impressed with that as with the other.

*Now tell me what everybody on campus and in the rest of the country has been talking about. Start from the beginning, with what happened when you sent the copy to Mr. Spielberg.*

"The original copy I sent to Mr. Spielberg on July 26 of this year, and with the copy I had an explanatory letter which mentioned how I had come to write the thing, how my friend, Sam Royall of the Williamsburg Press, organized it into the printed form of the booklet, and I mentioned in the letter that an 18-year-old student at the college, named Kim Wallace, who happens to be an English major, had

(Continued on p. 2)

### TV program relates to College and community

by Debbi Benham

This year at Christopher Newport College, a new type of TV program has emerged. Sponsored by Hampton Roads Cable Vision and CNC, the new program, entitled "Focus," offers a number of different topics that relate to the community and especially to the college itself.

---

The Times-Herald, Thursday, Oct. 7, 1982   17

# E.T. can star in prof's pamphlet

By LINDA GRIFFITH
Staff Writer

The controversy between Universal City Studios and a Christopher Newport College professor over "E.T. — The Extra-Terrestrial" has been resolved amicably.

The studio has decided not to pursue its threatened legal action against Dr. Albert Millar for his pamphlet, "E.T. — You're More Than A Movie Star."

"We have come to reasonable terms about the matter," said John G. Nuanes, an attorney with Universal.

Millar, chairman of the college English department, wrote the pamphlet listing 33 parallels between the movie character "E.T." and the life of Jesus Christ. In July, he wrote, "E.T." producer and director Steven Spielberg asking his permission to sell the pamphlet, and enclosed a copy.

Millar heard nothing until Sept. 22, when he received a telegram from Nuanes citing him for copyright and trademark infringement. Millar also was ordered to "surrender all unsold goods for destruction." Universal had bought all rights to the movie and its characters from Spielberg.

The professor had spent $300 to $400 to have the pamphlet printed but had sold only 23 of them for $1 each.

Since the story appeared in the Daily Press on Sept. 26, both Universal and Millar have been bombarded with calls and letters.

Newspapers coast to coast carried the story of Millar's plight via the Associated Press wire service, and he began receiving requests for the pamphlet from across the nation.

Millar has since been interviewed by media from all over the United States, a German wire service and an international news service.

A radio talk show originating in Ontario, Canada, interviewed Millar via telephone at midnight Tuesday. He also has been interviewed on two San Francisco radio programs, as well as programs in Sacramento, Salt Lake City and San Antonio.

National Public Radio and radio stations in Saskatchewan and Orlando will interview Millar next week.

Millar has received "300 or 400" letters and requests for the pamphlet.

Students had volunteered to set up a legal fund for Millar, who twice has been voted "Professor of the Year" by the students. Strangers writing to him also have sent money for his legal expenses and have asked for booklets, promising not to tell Universal Studios they bought one.

Among those requesting copies were the librarian for the Academy of Motion Picture Arts and Sciences; a representative of the Unification Church in Santa Clara, Calif.; and a researcher for "Saturday Night Live."

"Ninety-nine percent of it has been good," Millar said. "I'm just an absolute stranger to these people and they're pouring out their hearts." But some callers have suggested that "E.T. is demon-possessed and I shouldn't be dealing with it," he said.

Letters have been addressed to "E.T. Booklet, Newport News, Va." but have reached Millar either at home or at Christopher Newport College.

Millar and Jonathan S. Gibson III, an attorney who prepared Millar's response to Universal, will appear today on "Focus," a program produced at the college.

— 88 —

THE WASHINGTON POST    Monday, September 27, 1982    •••    B5

# E.T. and Jesus

## Virginia Professor Warned to Drop Booklet Comparing Them

NEWPORT NEWS, Sept. 26 (AP)—Universal City Studios has warned a Virginia college professor against continuing to distribute a pamphlet he produced comparing the movie "E.T.—The Extra-Terrestrial" with the life of Jesus.

Universal City Studios attorney John G. Nuanes notified Albert E. Millar Jr., chairman of the English Department at Christopher Newport College here, that sales of the booklet "without our consent . . . infringe upon the proprietary rights which we own."

Nuanes asked that the professor advise the studio he has "ceased all distribution and sale of any E.T. merchandise"; that he advise them of the number of copies sold and all revenues; and that he "advise us of all manufacturing sources."

"It's like using an atomic bomb to kill a flea," said Millar of the studio's telegram.

In his pamphlet, Millar, who teaches a course on the Bible as literature, listed 33 items in the movie he believes closely parallel the life of Jesus. He published the booklet—titled "E.T.—You're More Than a Movie Star"—in July at his own expense. He then wrote the movie's creator, Steven Spielberg, explaining his reasons and sent Spielberg a copy of the pamphlet. He has sold 23 of the booklets.

## Dr. Millar, you're more than an English professor

### Job interviews

Attention, seniors! Appointments should be made in the Placement Office, located in CC208, to interview with representatives from the following companies:

10/8–Central Fidelity Bank, Business/Communications/or English majors for management intern positions.

10/15–Legg, Mason, Wood, Walker, Inc. (Stock Broker). B.A. or B.S. Degree. Experience in sales for investment broker positions.

10/19–First Virginia Bank of Tidewater. Business majors for management intern positions.

— 89 —

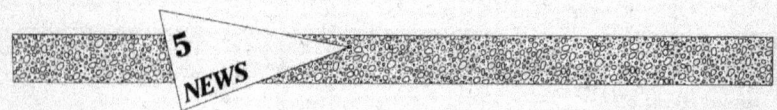

## Millar celebrates silver anniversary at CNC

**by Keith Delles**
*staff writer*

Wow! What a year for reflection and anniversary celebrations. This year we had the twentieth anniversary of the summer of love, the Rolling Stones touring again, The Who's reunion tour, Apollo 11's twentieth birthday, and Al Millar's twenty-fifth anniversary.

Al who?

Dr. Albert Millar, the beloved English professor here at CNC, is making his twenty-fifth year of service to the college and its students. Certainly since his arrival in September 1965, the past twenty-five have not been quiet years. Just ask movie director Steven Spielberg.

In what has perhaps become the most celebrated media event in CNC's history, Dr. Millar, in 1982, independently published a pamphlet entitled, "E.T." - You're More Than A Movie Star, drawing the ire from the lawyers at Spielberg's studio, Universal City. In the pamphlet, Dr. Millar had outlined thirty-three parallels between the E.T. character and Jesus Christ. He sold 25 pamphlets at a dollar each, although their printing cost him 400 dollars in expenses. Following an inter-

Dr. Millar, 1964.

view in the Daily Press, Universal City studios sent a telegram threatening legal action for "trademark infringement and unfair competition."

Dr. Millar's plight was subsequently chronicled in the Richmond Times-Dispatch, The Washington Post and Newsweek magazine. CBS Radio did a phone interview with him. The television show, "Entertainment Tonight", did a small segment on the imbroglio, and "Saturday Night Live" contacted him about their doing a skit on the subject. What did Dr. Millar think of the studio's attempt at legal retribution?

"It's like using an atomic bomb to kill a flea," quipped the jovial professor. Even Ed McMahon sent a letter of support for his cause.

Steven Spielberg was neutral on the matter despite the studio's objections. "I was born Jewish, I grew to become an atheist, and I don't know anything about this Jesus thing."

Then President of CNC, Dr. Andersen, told Dr. Millar, "Al whenever you give and interview whatever you do, just make sure they spell the college's name right!"

Another highlight of Dr. Millar's long tenure at CNC is the day he and a group of professors had lunch with Elizabeth Taylor when she spoke at the college. Dr. Millar's blue eyes bulge at the mention of this event.

"Oh Boy! I remember we had quiche for lunch and I kept staring at those violet eyes of hers. All I could think was, Wow, I'm in the presence of Cleopatra. Actually, she seemed really bored with the whole affair," recalls the slender professor.

The congenial, brown haired teacher has also been a leader in his twenty-five years. He served three terms as Chairman for the Department of English, and once as Chairman for the Department of Humanities in the school's infancy. He counts three Professor of the Year awards among his honors, but perhaps the greatest reward is his memories of the college's early years. Those memories kindle a warmth as he smiles, producing amiable crow's feet at his temples.

"Mr. Cunningham was the school's first president. He interviewed me where the computer lab is now. Would you like some butterscotch candy?" Dr. Millar inquires.

"No thanks," I reply.

"I offer them to freshmen when there's a bad crowd," he cackles. "Anyway, he must have saw some potential, so they gave me half of Dr. Sanderlin's class, put me in a corner classroom, and told me to keep my voice down. I got the nod for the job because I was a quarter-miler in college so I could also coach track. At the time there were only 150 pupils, and everyone parked around the flagpole."

Provoked at the thought of his original office, Dr. Millar clasps his hands together and humors himself about an anecdote from his first days. His office now lies to one extreme of the hallway on McMurran Hall's second floor.

**Continued on Page 9**

### Historic houses

*Courtesy of*
*The Chrysler Museum*

NORFOLK, VA—The Chrysler Museum's three historic houses will celebrate Military Month in November with special programs and free admission for all active duty and retired personnel and their dependents. During the month only a current military identification card is needed for admission at the Moses Myers or Willoughby-Baylor houses in downtown Norfolk and the Adam Thoroughgood House in Virginia Beach.

To initiate the festivities, the Thoroughgood House will host the Atlantic Fleet Band Woodwind Trio for concert at 2:00 p.m. on Sunday, November 5.

"Myers Men in the Military" will honor three generations of Myers veterans with a special tour of the Myers House at 1:00 and 3:00 p.m. on Veterans Day Saturday, November 11. Art LaBonte, curator at the War Memorial Museum of Virginia, will also give loading and firing demonstrations with two black powder guns. Both the flintlock musket and the percussion cap rifle he will use are reproductions made for the War Memorial Museum.

Both programs are free and open to the public. For further information contact The Chrysler Museum historic houses at

### ■ Millar

**Continued from Page 5**

"My current office was also my original office, but I was originally kicked out of it. The maintenance man, Mr. O'Dell, I believe his name was, saw me putting books up in my office on my first day. I was the youngest member of the faculty my first year, after all I was only twenty-five, so I was very youthful in appearance. The crew-cut kid. Well he thought it was bad for a student to hang around a teacher's office so he kicked me out. He's the one same maintenance man that thought Barry Wood, who's also form the English department, was the devil. He would make the sign of the cross with his fingers every time he saw him. Maybe he overheard Wood's coloration of the Anglo-Saxon language in one of his classes. All this was back in the sixties."

Among Dr. Millar's hobbies is his fondness for the beleaguered Dallas Cowboys. He gleams when he shows the letter from Roger Staubach he received in 1979 for sending the quarterback a Christmas booklet. "I used to drive an old 1966 Chevy painted Cowboy silver, but I

*by Matthew Howes, Photography Editor*
Dr. Millar and his E.T. collection.

got rid of it because I received too much flak from that 'other' team's fans."

Memories of his students are a source of pride for Dr. Millar. "I've always maintained that I would stack our best students up against anybody's. The abilities of our students has remained constant, although the students now have too many distractions. Of course back in '65 there was no Terrace to go have a drink. I keep on top of my students even thought I have an open attendance policy, which I guess I shouldn't have. I take yawn counts during my classes, keeping records for fifty and seventy-five minute classes. The records are continuously broken."

Dr. Al Millar had competition in his own family. His cousin, Dr. John Donald Millar, eradicated small pox and is currently the U.S. Assistant Surgeon General, and was once nominated for a Nobel Prize. Dr. Millar admits he fumbled around for awhile before he made his mark.

"I held six shipyard jobs where the happiest days were the days I quit. My first job offer out of college was for a VDI inspector in Alaska. After all that, I think I have found my niche here. I feel I was born to teach English and American Literature."

You will get no argument here, Al. Happy anniversary!

E-6 Richmond Times-Dispatch, Sun., Oct. 10, 1982

# College professor becomes celebrity after studio's threat over E.T. use

*Continued From First Page*

Joanthan S. Gibson III, "who broke out into a long laugh when he read it," Dr. Millar said. "He just laughed and laughed and said he couldn't believe the studio had taken such action. I almost loosened up myself then, but it was my name on the telegram."

During the next two weeks, Universal, through Nuanes, was apprised of the nature of Dr. Millar's publication. Thursday, the studio notified the professor that it had decided against any legal action and that he could continue to print and distribute his tract.

Dr. Millar said he believed the studio's decision not to pursue legal action was based, in part, on the large amount of publicity he has received in support of his pamphlet's message, primarily outside Virginia, through the Bible belt and on the West Coast.

"Mr. Nuanes admitted to us that he had never encountered such a barrage of protests and such a large number of people supporting me," Dr. Millar said.

Several national news organizations covered the legal confrontation and carried stories about the movie's Messianic overtones. Dr. Millar has been interviewed on radio talk shows in San Francisco, Salt Lake City, San Antonio, Texas, and Toronto. Stations in Saskatchewan and Orlando, Fla., have arranged for similar interviews with him next week.

His pamphlet has been mentioned on ABC's "Good Morning America" and on the syndicated satellite program "Entertainment Tonight." As a result, he has received 500 to 600 requests for copies of the pamphlet.

"What has happened to me is beyond my wildest dreams," Dr. Millar said. He has been teaching at the small, four-year state-supported liberal arts school since 1965. "I've been a mild-mannered English professor for years. This is the best thing that's ever happened to me. It's simply a trip. I've never been famous before.

"I'm not at all displeased by Christopher Newport College."

Dr. Millar said he recommends seeing the movie. He said he has watched people come out of the theater with tears on their face — "tears of joy."

"The movie offers some goodness. It offers hope and it just plain entertains."

Dr. Millar's perspective does not come from years as a moviegoer. Ironically, his religious background prevents him from seeing movies, except for a film on the coronation of Queen Elizabeth II and the film "The Ten Commandments," until he was out of high school.

"I've not seen many movies, but this one hit me. When I first saw it, I began to pick up on the similarities between E.T. and Jesus after the scene when E.T. heals Elliot's finger. I said to myself, 'There is potentially something very important here.' I didn't think anything Messianic until E.T.'s resurrection," he said.

Dr. Millar acknowledges that he cannot make a case for total parallels; they don't exist. But the similarities listed in his pamphlet total more than 33.

"I now know of about six others," he said.

One of the more striking similarities, he said, involves E.T.'s death.

"In the movie, the doctor pronounces him dead at 15:36, which is 3:36 p.m. That is especially significant, since the gospels place the death of Jesus on the cross at some brief time after the 'ninth hour' [Matthew 27:45]. The Hebrew day began at 6 a.m., so the ninth hour would have been 3 p.m.," Dr. Millar said.

Other similarities between E.T. and scriptural accounts of Jesus, he said, include E.T.'s prior extraterrestrial existence; that he came to little children; that he had occasion to feel rejected and forsaken on Earth; his healing those who loved him; his communication with "home;" his wearing a robe; his causing a plant virtually unnoticed to anyone outside Newport News.

"I had taken an advertisement out in The New York Times. It cost me about $30, but I got absolutely no responses," Dr. Millar said.

"Then, I bought an expensive ad. It cost $220 in The National Enquirer but it generated only 23 responses. So, when Nuanes sent me the telegram my total revenue was only $23 out of about $490 spent on advertising and printing. I never expected to make any money. I took out the ads just to try to get people to read what I had written." He has asked for one dollar each for copies to help cover his expenses.

"I guess I had created the most monumental failure in the history of writing," he said with a laugh. "But the publicity now has changed things. I don't know what I'm going to do next. I'm going to be on some more talk shows. I might print a second edition or print some of the key letters I've received or I might give some lectures."

But one thing is for certain, Dr. Millar's pamphlet, originally written as an outlet for his own beliefs, is attracting attention on the national level for its author and his college.

"Before, people seemed to think Christopher Newport College was in West Virginia or something, but now people all over the country know something about the college. It has a controversial English professor.

"I don't think I'm controversial," Dr. Millar said, his voice trailing off.

Our dad, Albert Millar with daughter Valerie

Dad with daughter Ginger

Val, Gin, Dad, and Heather

Heather E. Millar, Ph.D., MBA, is an adjunct faculty member, researcher and principal/owner of Millar Strategies, LLC, a SWAM-certified consulting business. Heather's research interests include higher education trends, including policy developments and public administration, with specific interests in governmental decision-making, institutional theory of organizations, and the theory of bounded rationality. Heather received her undergraduate degree from Randolph-Macon College, her MBA from Virginia Commonwealth University (VCU), and her Ph.D. from the VCU L. Douglas Wilder School of Government and Public Affairs.

Heather in her Halloween costume circa 1983.

www.ingramcontent.com/pod-product-compliance
Lightning Source LLC
Chambersburg PA
CBHW052033030426
42337CB00027B/4988